Get Your Pretense On!

THE URBAN MINISTRY INSTITUTE, A MINISTRY OF WORLD IMPACT, INC.

GET YOUR PRETENSE ON!

Living as a Citizen and Ambassador of the Kingdom of God

Rev. Dr. Don L. Davis

TUMI Press · 3701 East 13th Street North · Wichita, Kansas 67208

I dedicate this book to every believer
who has had the courage to "get their pretense on,"
living by God's declaration of who they are and
what they possess, even in the face of doubt,
opposition and persecution . . .

To those who walk by faith and not by sight,

Who confess their true identity in Christ
in the face of the world's rejection and lies,

Who stand their ground against the strongholds of the enemy,

Who hold the line in the truth in Jesus, no matter what.

To all of you, I dedicate this book.

And without faith it is impossible to please him,
for whoever would draw near to God must believe that he exists
and that he rewards those who seek him.

~ Hebrews 11.6 ~

Table of Contents

Appendices

About the Author

Rev. Dr. Don L. Davis is the Executive Director of The Urban Ministry Institute and a Senior Vice President of World Impact. He attended Wheaton College and Wheaton Graduate School, and graduated *summa cum laude* in both his B.A.(1988) and M.A. (1989) degrees, in Biblical Studies and Systematic Theology, respectively. He earned his Ph.D. in Religion (Theology and Ethics) from the University of Iowa School of Religion.

As the Institute's Executive Director and World Impact's Senior Vice President, he oversees the training of urban missionaries, church planters, and city pastors, and facilitates training opportunities for urban Christian workers in evangelism, church growth, and pioneer missions. He also leads the Institute's extensive distance learning programs and facilitates leadership development efforts for organizations and denominations like Prison Fellowship, the Evangelical Free Church of America, and the Church of God in Christ.

Dr. Davis has served as professor at a number of academic institutions, including Wheaton College, St. Ambrose University, the Houston Graduate School of Theology, the University of Iowa School of Religion, and the Robert E. Webber Institute of Worship

Studies. He has authored a number of books, including *The Capstone Curriculum*, TUMI's premiere sixteen-module distance education seminary instruction, *Sacred Roots: A Primer on Retrieving the Great Tradition*, *Black and Human: Rediscovering King as a Resource for Black Theology and Ethics*, *Building Bridges, and Scaling Walls: Learning the Art of Edifying Dialogue*.

Don and his wife, Beth, married in February 1975, and together they have three children (one deceased), and four grandchildren.

Preface

The Golden Rule of Good Pretense, by Don Davis

Act every day just like
God done told you you actually is,
Cause' if you fail to act
On what He say you be
Then you'll never become
what you's always been from the beginnin'!

This book is inspired by a concept unpacked by the great apologist, C. S. Lewis in his pithy and helpful little book, *Mere Christianity*. In that insightful text, Lewis explains his notion of the relationship between bad pretense and good pretense in a chapter entitled "Let's Pretend," given through his brief exposition of the actual language used in the Lord's Prayer. Essentially, Lewis suggests that no one can relate to the Lord without actually pretending to be what the Father claims you are, though all evidence and internal emotional confirmation argues to the contrary. In other words, we are who we are because God says so, and the Christian life is lived largely on the basis of accepting that, even though, on the surface, things don't seem to agree with God's claims of our rightful identity. Such is my poor commentary on his brilliant analysis. Below is a portion of his amazing argument:

> Its very first words are "Our Father." Do you now see what those words mean? They mean quite frankly, that you are putting yourself in the place of a son of God. To put it bluntly, you are dressing up as Christ. If you like, you are pretending. Because, of course, the moment you realize what the words mean, you realize that you are not a son of God. You are not being like The Son of God, whose will and interests are at one with those of the Father: you are a bundle of self-centered fears, hopes, greeds, jealousies, and self-conceit, all doomed to death. So that, in a way, this dressing up as Christ is a piece of outrageous cheek. But the odd thing is that He has ordered us to do it.
>
> Why? What is the good of pretending to be what you are not? Well, even on the human level, you know, there are two kinds of pretending. There is a bad kind, where the pretense is there instead of the real thing; as when a man pretends he is going to help you instead of really helping you. *But there is also a good kind, where the pretense leads up to the real thing* [italics mine].
>
> When you are not feeling particularly friendly but know you ought to be, the best thing you can do, very often, is to put on a friendly manner and behave as if you were a nicer person than you actually are. And in a few minutes, as we have all noticed, you will be really feeling friendlier than you were. Very often the only way to get a quality in reality is to start behaving as if you had it already. That is why children's games are so important. They are always pretending to be grown-ups – playing soldiers, playing shop. But all the time, they are hardening their muscles and sharpening their wits, so that the pretense of being grown-up helps them to grow up in earnest.[1]

This idea of pretending your way into who you really are –
"hardening" muscles and "sharpening" wits – is a fundamental
disposition of the Christian life. This text seeks to make this
plain. We who believe in Christ have been grafted into a Story
so big that the entire universe and all of time will not contain
it. We are now, by faith, recipients of the Kingdom's authority
and rule, baptized by the Spirit as members into the body of
Christ, the pillar and ground of the truth, so says the apostle
Paul. We have been granted an entirely new identity with a
new nature, set free from the futility of empty religion and
legalism, all in order that we might represent Christ in this
world as his ambassadors and agents.

Now, through the Spirit's leading, we are commissioned to represent
his interests in our own unique, special web of relationships, given
the privilege to pray, and proclaim the Good News of Christ to
our family members, friends, and associates. In these last few
sentences is the entire plan of this little book, which I hope can
encourage you to "get your pretense on," as we say in the
neighborhood where I currently live and minister.

Everything is at stake in our ability to claim as our own those
gifts, privileges, status, inheritances, and blessings God says he
has provided us in Christ. No one will be able to enjoy the rich
depths of Christ's salvation blessings if they refuse to go against
their feelings, circumstances, and "odds" to cling simply to the
truth as it is in Christ. That is the key to Christian identity and
to fruitfulness in Christian ministry.

This is a theological work, not a tactical manual. I may be a
dinosaur because I believe the Bible doctrine is the key to an
adventurous, wonderful, and meaningful life. You cannot *live*
well if you do not *see* well. The focus of this book is *how you see
yourself and the world*. Its basic conviction is that, once you
come to understand who God is, what he is doing in the world,

and what part you can play in his great adventure of rescue and reversal, then you will be ready to get going and to apply yourself in the direction he leads. Only *after* you see, can you "get your pretense on" and start acting like you truly are who he says you are.

Of course, too, this is a work that had to be written, but needed to end (if you understand my meaning). In other words, each of the chapters in this work could easily take its own unique text, with its argument and explanation. Consider this a primer of the kind of mindset that every effective ambassador and agent of Jesus Christ must have in order to affect the kind of change that the Spirit would have her do in the situation where he has placed her. It is a combination of grand epic ideas and practical daily tasks. It covers the entirety of the biblical vision, but drills down on what it means to be a middle-schooler for Jesus.

This is, of course, the way it is with all Christian subjects. Theologically, the themes are dipped into the greatest story ever told, but practically, they relate to the meeting that we have with friends or family tomorrow night. Be flexible in your modes of reading it; sometimes it will require you to put on a prophet's mantle and think with the sages over the great issues of our time (see Appendix, *The Story of God*), and other times you simply have to understand why a 155-pound police officer can make an 18-ton diesel truck grind to a halt (see Appendix, *Understanding Leadership as Representation*). C. S. Lewis instinctively knew that nothing can be truly learned in Christian thought and experience without this need to experience good pretense, that is, to act like you are who God says you are, no matter how you feel or how things look. Consider this book a field manual for good pretense.

In some ways, this work is a collection of sermons, presentations, and essays, all of which together represent a theological constellation of six of the most fundamental concepts I believe are necessary to

Christian discipleship and ministry. They are integrally connected. The themes in each of the chapters have been preached, proclaimed, and presented dozens of times in every possible venue, all with great verve and energy. (What I lacked in light I made up in sweat!) Hopefully, the integration of the themes will be apparent and clear; any lack of clarity, I claim as my own.

One brief comment should be made about the Appendices. We have provided the charts at the end of this book in order to strengthen and illustrate the insights shared in the text. As a visual thinker and a metaphor creator, it is difficult for me not to visualize truths even as I explain them. When a particular appendix is relevant to a discussion, I will mention it in context. Beyond this, though, I have also included several graphics intended to help you "come to grips" with the truths discussed in the book. Please take ample time to look at each one of them carefully, letting them offer further wisdom and reflection on the importance of these key truths.

Remember that this text was written for a gathering of our TUMI alumni and students to challenge them to mobilize themselves for a new aggressive push to fulfill the Great Commission. Read it within that light, and you will see it is a call to arms, all based on our ability to "get our pretense on" (Lewis's *Let's Pretend*) and to challenge a generation to start acting like we are whom God says we are. I trust that it will have a similar impact upon your heart and life, challenging you to play your part in the greatest Story ever told.

Your contribution is critical to our overall and global success. In the end, a Christian is a person who has come to believe God's claims and affirmations about the nature and meaning of life and the world more than anything else, even her own conclusions and judgments. By no means! Let God be true though every one were a liar, as it is written, "That you may be justified in your words, and prevail when you are judged" (Rom. 3.4). Let God be justified in his words, and may he prevail in all arguments where we are judged.

We still wait to see the impact of a few people who actually take the Word of God seriously. I choose to be one of those people, even though, as Lewis declares, to do so is "a piece of outrageous cheek." This text calls you, the reader, to join me in this "cheekiness." We are whom God says we are, and we can do what God says we can do. This is the thesis of this book.

Don Davis
March 2018

CHAPTER 1

The Greatest Story in the Word:
Seeing Things as They Really Are

This book is about you learning how to act like the person that God says you are, even though you don't feel like it, and the situation you find yourself in seems to contradict it.

Understanding who you are in Christ and living in a manner that corresponds to it – what in this book I am calling "getting your pretense on" – demands that you begin to take your cues for how you should live from what you know about the Story of God, given in Scripture. That Story, the truest and most final story of all, has a lot to do with fantastical and epic stories itself. It demands that you see things differently to understand yourself and what life is about.

Interestingly, the Story of God in the Bible is just like a fairy tale, or a comic book story. *What!? Am I kidding?* What in the world does the biblical Story of God's love in Christ have in common with comic book adventures, hero journeys, or fairy tales?

Okay, sure. On the one hand, God's Story and comics have very *little at all* to do with each other. Comics and fairy stories are fictions, the product of an author's imagination, laying out dreamed-up worlds and characters which do not exist to fight evil that is not present.

Yet, the Bible, on the other hand, is the divinely inspired record of God's saving work in creation, Israel, and Christ. Its vision of creation and destiny read just like a fairy tale, the kind where God almighty will restore all things that humanity lost and twisted, integrating it back under his rule. Quite literally, we *shall* live "happily ever after." This narrative is epic and marvelous, but it is also historically accurate and spiritually vital. The events and happenings did and will take place, as all who truly believe demonstrate by their devotion to its hero, Jesus of Nazareth, our Lord and Christ.

So, to be a believer in the Kingdom of God, to hold to Jesus Christ as Messiah and Lord, does involve seeing things differently. To be a disciple is to see things as God does. And here is where the Bible and fairy tale seem to line up. As J. R. R. Tolkien said, in the biblical tale of God's love in Christ legend and truth, fairy tale and history, myth and reality come together.

In the eucatastrophic tale (i.e., "good catastrophe" story), the grace of goodness seems to laser in at the last minute, ending doom and restoring the just to their rightful places.

> The consolation of fairy-stories, the joy of the happy ending: or more correctly of the good catastrophe, the sudden joyous "turn" (for there is no true end to any fairy-tale): this joy, which is one of the things which fairy-stories can produce supremely well, is not essentially "escapist." . . . In its fairy-tale – or otherworldly – setting, it is a sudden and miraculous grace: never to be counted on to recur. It does not deny the existence of dyscatastrophe, of sorrow and failure: the possibility of these is necessary to the joy of deliverance; it denies (in the face of much evidence, if you will) universal final defeat and in so far

is evangelium, giving a fleeting glimpse of Joy, Joy beyond the walls of the world, poignant as grief.[2]

While all great hero and fairy stories mirror the Bible's grand story in reversing the way things appear and turn out, they differ from Scripture in one mighty respect. The biblical tale of redemption and restoration is also absolutely true; as amazing, as remarkable, as awe-inspiring as it is, it is both a grand catastrophe and true to its core. And no other narrative of the world can claim to be both eucatastrophic and true other than the Story of God in Christ.

It is not difficult to imagine the peculiar excitement and joy that one would feel, if any specially beautiful fairy-story were found to be "primarily" true, its narrative to be history, without thereby losing the mythical or allegorical significance that it had possessed. It is not difficult, for one is not called upon to try and conceive anything of a quality unknown. The joy would have exactly the same quality . . . as the joy which the "turn" in a fairy story gives: such joy has the very taste of primary truth. . . . It looks forward (or backward: the direction in this regard is unimportant) to the Great Eucatastrophe. The Christian joy, the Gloria, is of the same kind; but it is pre-eminently . . . high and joyous. Because this story is supreme; and it is true. Art has been verified. God is the Lord, of angels, and of men – and of elves. Legend and History have met and fused.[3]

You see, in the world of all hero stories and fairy tales (as it is in the biblical tale) nothing truly is as it on the surface appears to be.

To be sure, to read comic books and fairy stories in the right way, you must believe that what you are looking at ain't all there is out there, because nothing is as it appears to be.

The Strange World of Transformation in Comic Stories

Peter Parker, the shy photographer swallowed up by his angry editor, living with his aunt in a small house, is in fact the Amazing Spider Man. Clark Kent, who grew up in little Smallville, and who works as an easy-to-forget reporter, is nothing less than Kal-El of Krypton, known more familiarly to us as Superman. And Bruce Wayne, the so-called playboy and wealthy spoiled brat who wastes away his time and energy on pleasure and selfishness, is in fact the caped Crusader, the Batman.

You see, in hero and fairy stories, you can't judge a thing on the basis of how it looks; you've got to go deeper down, further in, to the real meaning of the thing. In a comic book adventure, you simply can never comprehend the full nature of a thing by judging it purely on the face of it.

In fairy stories, a frog may be a prince, a beautiful temptress a wicked witch, a po' girl in the basement may be the future princess of the kingdom, or a small-town boy may be Superman. In fairy stories, it is prudent to kiss every frog you encounter, because you never know if a prince might happen to be dwelling inside it.

Frederick Buechner in *Telling the Truth: The Gospel as Tragedy, Comedy, and Fairy Tale* says this of fairy tales:

> Beasts talk and flowers come alive and lobsters quadrille in the world of the fairy tale, and nothing is apt to be what it seems. And if this is true of the creatures that the hero meets on his quest, it is true also of the hero himself who at any moment may be changed into a beast or a stone or a king or have his heart turned to ice. Maybe above all they are tales about transformation where all creatures are revealed in the end as what they truly are – the ugly duckling becomes a great white swan, the frog is revealed to be a prince, and the beautiful but wicked queen

is unmasked at last in her ugliness. They are tales of transformation where the ones who live happily ever after, as by no means everybody does in fairy tales, are transformed into what they have it in them at their best to be.[4]

The Story of God: The Lord's Tale of Grace and Glory

Indeed, this is where the tales and the Tale of the Scriptures hold similar attributes.

To be a Christian is to believe that Supermans do live in Smallville, shy reporters can be Spiderman, and lowly toads may be shining princes, one kiss away from a new future. To be a disciple of Jesus is to be in the business of kissing frogs and nursing ugly ducklings, for nothing is as it appears to be.

In the Story of God, like fairy tales, the stakes are unbelievably high and the conflict is cosmic and universal. God will elect to redeem his creation, purely out of love and grace, and to rescue out of Adam's line a people who will live forever in a new heavens and new earth which he himself will recreate. Like in a fairy story, he will provide an intervention of grace and love so sufficient that it will take on the evil and chaos that have ruined creation, and with a single act of sacrifice, destroy death and corruption forever. And he will offer this free deliverance to any and all who believe in his Son, the true hero of the Story, whose people will serve him in a Kingdom where God is glorified forever.

Have you heard it? Do you know the Story? How can we so encounter this true tale of God's love and grace in such as way as to be transformed by it forever?

True Discipleship: How God's Story Shapes Our Lives

The Scriptures lay out for all to see the divinely authorized Story of the triune God – in his wondrous acts in creation, his people

Israel, the Incarnation, and the Church. God the Father Almighty is the divine author of the Story, Jesus of Nazareth is the Story's hero, the Holy Spirit is the Story's narrator and producer, and the Bible is its script and record. This Story represents the Church's essential biblical faith. God tells and narrates this Story in the Bible, and as we read it we come to understand that Story as God's divinely authorized narration of his wondrous work of salvation.

Moreover, the Church of God is the Story's protector and guardian. As we walk by faith in the Son of God we prove ourselves to be the Story's living, present-day continuation – amazingly, God's community becomes the place where God's kingdom reign is seen and experienced.

This great Story of God's love and life becomes, then, our master narrative through which we see the world, and by which we fulfill our mission. In the Church's theology, she reflects on the Story's truth and glory, and in her worship, she sings, preaches, and reenacts the milestones of the Story. Through her Gospel and baptism, the Church shares the Story with the lost. When new converts repent and believe in Jesus, they are incorporated into God's great family, a community where these new believers learn the rules of our faith and walk in the ways of the Nazarene. In their repentance and baptism they embrace an entirely new identity as new characters in the Story of God in Jesus. To join the family is simultaneously to embrace the Story.

Likewise, in her spiritual formation, the Church embodies, indwells, and acts out the Story. As she practices her disciplines for the purpose of spiritual formation, she participates as a major actor in the Story. Through the charisms given to all Christians by the Spirit in authentic community, every Christian can take his/her role as a twenty-first-century actor in God's cosmic drama. And, as the Church testifies and bears witness of the Good News, she fleshes the Story out for all to see. In her preaching and outreach she boldly communicates and demonstrates the Story through acts of hospitality and generosity, and through evangelism and mission. Our aim is simple. *We as believers must strive to so live out the Story before the lost in order that, through our words and deeds, they may learn of its wonder and be attracted to its gracious invitation.*

Truly, then, the Church is the people of the Story. In every way the Story shapes her identity, inspires her worship, and fuels her passions for God and love for others. (We will discuss in depth the role of the church in relation to the Kingdom Story of God in chapter three).

Once upon a Time: The Biblical Story Told

You can't appreciate the scope and power of the Christian narrative of the world until you understand and encounter it. It is so remarkable that it is told rightly only when told with joy and power. Let us here now, then, summarize the Story, tell it plain and good in the somewhat dry theological language of the schools, but still a wondrous and powerful way to hear it. In the few paragraphs that follow, I will lay out the Tale of tales so you can see its power and insight.

A Sovereign God Creates the Worlds

The Bible begins with the creation of the universe by a sovereign and triune God, Father, Son, and Holy Spirit, who existed before all else, from everlasting to everlasting. This perfect God, the Lord God Almighty, dwelt in eternal glory – our God lacked nothing before he chose to create the universe.

Based purely on his loving-kindness and determination to create a universe that would reflect his glory, this great God decided to act. In his eternal counsels and wisdom, he decided to make a universe where his workmanship would be displayed. He decided, too, to make a world where human beings, made in his own likeness and image, could dwell in paradise, and share in the fullness of his creation's beauty.

A Rebellious Prince Creates Chaos in the Universe
In spite of God making creation and human beings perfect, his creation was thrown into chaos through the deception of a rebellious angelic prince, Satan. Through his prideful deception, and his intent to overthrow God's Kingdom, he tempted the first human pair in the Garden. Refusing to listen to and obey the Lord's command, they elected to rebel against God's will – they refused to acknowledge his lordship.

To humankind's regret, Adam and Eve disobeyed God's clear command, and rejected his good will. Through their disobedience they elected to live according to their own pride and greed, and were cast into darkness. Because of their lust for power the entire creation was cursed, and chaos now entered into God's creation. The entire universe would be scarred and ruined by their selfish and ill-conceived fall.

Separated from God and subject to death, the first human pair was banished from God's perfect paradise. Sadly, Adam and Eve were doomed to live in creation now cursed on account of their sin. The consequences of their acts were terrible and devastating. Because of their fall, they would now be forced to end their miserable existence in physical death. All their heirs would share the same fate of doom and death, with no hope of deliverance or transformation.

The Triune God Covenants to Save His Creation
Thanks be to God! This horrible condition of humankind would not have the last word. Based purely on his eternal love and compassion, this great triune God covenanted to send a divine warrior for the sake of creation's and humankind's rescue.

This "seed of the woman" would overthrow the "seed of the serpent" (Satan), and ultimately defeat all the powers that harmed God's good creation. This seed, this Deliverer, would crush the skull of the serpent who deceived the first human pair, and bring lasting eternal remedy to the chaos and curse plaguing the universe. The price of redemption, though, would be high: the One to come would also be bruised by the serpent, upon the warrior's heel.

Through his oversight and sovereign will, through his covenants and divine leading, God entered as an actor into human history. Rather than merely telling the Story, our God became its central Actor and main Hero: he himself determined by direct participation to make an end of sin, destroy the serpent, restore creation, and draw out of the earth a people for his own possession.

And so, God made a covenant with Abraham, and ratcheted down the physical lineage of the Seed to come. He renewed the covenant with Abraham's son, Isaac, and then established which tribe in the earth the Redeemer would be born into. He renewed the covenant with Jacob, Isaac's son, and delivered the nation of Israel, Jacob's heirs, from Egypt. Through mighty miracles and awesome signs, the Lord through Moses rescued his great nation from Pharaoh at the Exodus. Through Joshua he brought them into his Promised Land, and through the judges he delivered his people from their enemies. He elected Jesse's son, the young David, to be champion over Goliath, and through him established the lineage of the King, the one destined to rule forever in God's restored Kingdom.

Despite all of God's awesome miracles and mighty wonders, tragically, his people still rebelled foolishly against him. They oppressed their neighbors, disobeyed his covenants, and worshiped false gods. Despite numerous warnings given through the prophets, they persisted in their idolatry and sin, and ultimately were taken into exile (i.e., the northern tribes into Assyria, and the southern tribes into Babylon).

Though they deserved his just judgment, our God refused to forget his promise to their fathers. He would keep his word in the Garden, to Abraham, to Moses, and to David. In his mercy and covenant faithfulness, he would bring from exile a remnant of his people – to keep his promise, and to be true to himself, and his word of redemption for the world.

The Greatest Mystery of All: The Word Becomes Flesh

In the fullness of time, God set into motion the events which would lead to the birth of the babe of the Virgin Mary. From the line of David, and in sync with his great promises given through the prophets, God Almighty sent his Son into the world. By God's high decree, his one and only Son would enter into his creation. Being conceived of the Holy Spirit, and born of the Virgin Mary, God's true Son and our Savior became incarnate. The same Word that was with God and was God entered into the realm of human life, taking on the form of a servant, and was found in the likeness of humankind, taking into himself our brokenness, vulnerability, and suffering.

As the Last Adam who would undo the damage caused by the first Adam's disobedience, Jesus of Nazareth fulfilled the Father's moral will. Through his words he displayed the Kingdom's wisdom, and through his works he displayed the Kingdom's power. Through his exorcisms he displayed the Kingdom's authority, and through his miracles he demonstrated the Kingdom's release from evil, the Curse, sickness, sin – and even death. Neither Hades, nor death, nor disease, nor the devil could withstand his clear and true representation of the Father. In him the Kingdom was inaugurated; the very word sworn to Abraham became visible for all to see.

At the climax of his life, he submitted himself and became obedient to death, even death on a Roman Cross. In a remarkable show of courage and grace, Jesus the Nazarene went to Calvary, freely taking on the sin and rebellion of humankind, suffering as the Lamb of God, the victim suffering on our behalf. Voluntarily, our Lord gave up his life and died, paying the penalty of our sin, and destroying the devil and his works. In his dying he eliminated death, and in his suffering he restored Creation back to the Father – and to the Father's children.

After three days, the Messiah of God, Jesus of Nazareth, rose again from the dead, bringing hope and new life to God's entire creation, and to all humankind. Now, because of the Son's obedience and his victory over the Curse and the Grave, all creatures will receive the blessings of God's great salvation. Now, with the curse rescinded and the battle won, it is certain that God will create afresh a new heavens and new earth. Calvary fulfills the apocalyptic anthem: "all things are made new!" The Lord Jesus Christ himself becomes the beginning of a new creation, the literal firstborn from among the dead!

Forty days after his resurrection, the Lord Jesus Christ ascended to the right hand of God as Lord of all. As Victor over hell and death, he is exalted to be Head of the Church, and Lord of the harvest. Having presently received all power from the Father, he with the Father sends the Holy Spirit to the earth. Jesus has won the victory, and at this very moment he is distributing the blessings of his saving work on the Cross.

The Spirit of God comes upon the little company of disciples at Pentecost, and now through his divine regeneration and adoption of the believing, he establishes the Church. This new people of God represents the literal presence of the Kingdom in this world. With their Spirit-indwelt gatherings of faith, they show themselves to be the family of the Father, the body of Christ, and the temple of the Spirit on earth for all to see and to marvel at.

As the Church tells the Story of God's eternal covenant faithfulness in Jesus, the Holy Spirit draws the lost to the Lord. Now through his ministry, he is calling men, women, boys, and girls from every kindred, tongue, people, and nation into union with Christ by faith. Through his sealing and anointing, the Holy Spirit is drawing new members into Christ's body. In their repentance and faith they make their election sure, being baptized by faith, accepting the Good News of Christ's grace, and by being incorporated into his Church. Regardless of culture, gender, class, or place, these believing disciples are welcomed into the one, holy, catholic, and apostolic community of the King.

Awaiting the Return of the King to Reign

In our day we enter into the very last days of the Story. Soon and very soon, when the work of proclamation is finished, God will direct his Son to return to earth. Soon the visions of the prophets will come to pass, and the word of the apostles will come true. The Lord Jesus Christ, who began his work in the Incarnation and secured it upon the Cross, will establish God's Kingdom throughout the entire universe.

All of God's creation will experience the glorious freedom of God's children. Jesus will return, judge the world in righteousness, and then, under God's direction, establish his glorious and eternal reign. Satan and his minions will be judged, and the world will be transformed. The glory of God will be revealed, and all creation will rejoice. Sorrow, disease, death, and shame will be banished forever, and the kingdom of this world will become the Kingdom of our Lord and of his Christ – and he will reign forever.

This great Story will end with the Father receiving the Kingdom from the hand of his Son, and God will ultimately be our All-in-all. This outline of the events to come represents just a snapshot of our hope and certain future. Because of the love of God, the grace of our Lord Jesus Christ, and the communion of the Spirit, those who believe will live "happily ever after." We are destined for the throne – we who believe will serve our God, transformed by grace, empowered forever with incorruptible bodies just like our Lord's own glorious body, to bring glory to him always. In his new heavens and new earth, all things will forever glorify God as Lord. Nothing can prevent this Story's future from being accomplished, for the Lord himself has sworn it.

Come, Join the Story of God

Can you begin to feel the excitement of this amazing tale of God's grace and love? In a world gone mad with power, lust, and greed, the Holy Spirit calls the Church to be faithful to God's biblical revelation of Jesus of Nazareth. This same clear, simple tale of God's awesome grace is recorded in the Bible, summarized in the creeds, and passed down faithfully through the centuries by the Church.

Despite the issues and challenges we face today in this world, this Story continues to draw the lost to its Good News. This great tale of Jesus of Nazareth, the Story's champion and hero, is as fresh today as when the disciples told it after the resurrection. Nothing has changed in the Story. The God who spawned it still loves us, the Savior who redeems us by his death still can save. The Spirit who fell on the first company of disciples can still empower us today. What then, do we need to do?

The answer is clear. We only need to hear this Story afresh, to sense its truthfulness and power once more, to recover the same true message that the consensus of the ancient Church fleshed out. The great traditions of Orthodoxy, Catholicism, Anglicanism, and the Protestant Reformation have defended it, artists have drawn it, musicians sung it, and missionaries brought it. All we need to do is rediscover it, and embody it once more.

Let us ask God to give us the courage to re-embrace this Narrative of narratives, this grand tale of God's matchless love. When all is said and done, it is a simple story after all. It can be understood through Scripture's testimony of creation, and seen in the great acts of God throughout the history of Israel. This great tale comes to its climax in the incarnation, death and resurrection of Jesus. Now, by faith, you can enter the Story, too.

If you look around, you won't fail to see many weird and fanciful competing master narratives seeking our allegiance. Religious jihad, political ideology, and strange philosophies all try to explain the meaning of the universe – where we came from and where we are going. For us who believe and follow Jesus of Nazareth, however, we need only hold onto the biblical Story. This Story of God's saving acts in Christ for us is the narration of the entire universe. In its retelling, enactment, and embodiment, the truth about all things is made plain.

All the big questions of life can be understood through the inspired telling of God's acts in history. You begin to understand who you are the more you come to understand what God is doing, and how you fit into it. Every time we go to church or Bible study or prayer meeting, we have an opportunity to rehearse the truth about God's great Story, and about his salvation in Jesus. You see, we are a continuation of the Story; we are that people who live out the Story in our confession, our songs and worship, our discipleship, and our testimony about Jesus. He is more than a tale; he is our very life and hope. Getting your pretense on is no fanciful or fantastic idea; when you act in a manner that befits and corresponds to this Story, you are literally being what you were always meant to be!

Our New Vocation: Have You Kissed Any Frogs Lately?

As you move through this text, you are going to learn what it means to act consistent with God's Word, even though its truths are so big and so amazing you'll feel like it is honestly "too good to be true." But you need to fight the temptation and never forget, that this Story is true! Still, if you ever find yourself in a fairy story, you ought to kiss as many frogs in it as you can, because, as said before, a frog may actually be a crown prince, turned into a frog through the dark magic of beautiful temptress/wicked witch. To be safe, if you understand the fairy story, you'd better be ready to give a frog a smooch, because you may never know what might emerge from that kiss.

To be a Christian is to understand that, soon and very soon, a new world is about to dawn. As active players on God's stage, we live the rhythm of the divine calendar. The Bible, our Scriptures, tells the account of the canonical story of the Triune God. It is his story, and my story is a part of his grand tale. He created and he promised rescue. He called his people and he sent his Son. He is calling his people to him, and he will recreate the heavens and earth. In the end, we must see this is God's story, and we are members of his plot, by faith.

Here is the wisdom of the ancient Church. They believed this Story with their hearts, in spite of persecution from without and heresy from within. They guarded the Story recorded in Scripture, and summarized it in their Rules of Faith. They recited it in their Apostles' and Nicene[5] Creeds, and trained their candidates for baptism and leaders within its truths.[6] This Story shaped their lives, for they believed it to be true. And, in agreement with them, we also hold it to be true and to be the Story which gives meaning to the entire universe.

In this Story, all who believe that Jesus is the Christ can be transformed from frogs to princes and princesses, through the power of the Spirit and faith in the Gospel. In a world that is dizzy with dozens of contradictory, competing stories, we who believe must now rediscover the Story of God in Christ as the final story of all things, the center of our lives, and the heart of our mission.

TUMI's Singular Passion: Raising Up God-storytellers
From the very founding of The Urban Ministry Institute, we have dedicated ourselves in all our curriculum and training to raise up a generation of storytellers and story-indwellers who can preach, teach, sing, and embody the Story with power before their family members, neighbors, associates, and strangers. Our entire enterprise in our Sacred Roots motif is to help urban dwellers learn and be transformed by the simple Story of God's love, the tale of a caring, sovereign Lord who became one of us, who took on our nature and entered our human history to redeem creation and a people for himself.

This striking, awesome, and true Story can bring revival to our weak and struggling churches. If we hold on to the Story as it is told in the Bible, summarized in the Creeds, and embodied in the Great Tradition[7] we will multiply disciples. You see, the Story is true, powerful, and it is ours. No communion or tradition owns it – it belongs to the entire Church, and will transform all who are willing to give themselves over to its wonder and glory.

I believe that if you really get our Story (or rather, if our Story really gets you!), you'll be inclined to go hunt for some frogs to kiss, or some ugly ducklings to raise, or even a few Cinderellas to liberate. In the Kingdom Story, as in all great stories, you simply can never know who it is you have encountered, or what is truly happening. Things are more than what they appear to be. Dead messiahs rise again, and meek disciples wind up inheriting the earth. Can you see it?

This is where we must begin to get our pretense on. It is here we begin with forging identity. It does not start with us, our gifts, talents, desires or dreams. It begins with the Father and his Son, with the Spirit's telling of *his triune Story*, the tale of love and grace and rescue. No person can possibly know what their life is about or what life means if they ignore God's telling of the one, true, and final Story of the creation, and his design to bring it back under his rule.

In God's Story, the weak shame the strong, and the poor are rich in faith and heirs of the Kingdom. In God's Story, the first will be last and the last first. In God's Story, to be great in the Kingdom is to be the servant of all. Everything is topsy-turvy, upside-down, inside-out. To succeed in the Kingdom, you've got to be prepared to see things in a new way, to let the Story change the way in which you see and understand everything. Story-tellers and Story-indwellers all know how to kiss frogs in such a way as to see some princes liberated out of them. The life of the prince is there; you need only give it a smooch to unlock the power.

In the end, you simply ought not trust any so-called champions of the Kingdom who do not have warts on their lips, or don't raise ugly ducklings for a living. They're not legit.

I wonder – have you kissed any frogs lately? Join the Story, and let your life be made whole, and be transformed. Believe me, as you better learn the Story, you'll come to enjoy kissing frogs, in time.

Comprehending who we are and what we have been called to be and do in life demands that we figure out what God is doing. In the next chapter we will discuss how this magnificent Story of God comes out in the language of *reversal*, the main pulse of the Kingdom of God in the teaching and ministry of Jesus of Nazareth.

CHAPTER 2
The Principle of Reversal and
the Upside-Down Kingdom of God

As mentioned in the first chapter, the only way to comprehend ourselves rightly is to get our mental frameworks right, that is, we must to come to see things, as it were, from God's point of view. The truth of the matter is this: *we do not live our lives on the basis of what really is, but rather on the basis of how we think it is!* Of all God's creatures, human beings cannot live well without possessing a clear reason for doing so; we simply have to have a purpose for our lives that makes sense to us, integrates the various pieces of our lives into some kind of story that makes sense and is clear. We come to live our lives on the basis of a perspective and vision that we adopt, our own personal "explanation" of why we are here, who we are, and how the world works. We desire coherence – we all desperately want our lives to make sense.

People, of necessity, tend to operate according to their interpretive frameworks: we live, as one commentator puts it, as "walking worldviews," creatures that make sense of things through the story that we tell ourselves. Every human existence is basically lived in a "story-ordered world," where our families, relationships, and culture help us to compose a story, a worldview, which helps us to answer the big questions of our lives. Our searching and answers to the basic questions of life provide us with a blueprint whereby we come to understand how the world works, and how we ought to define our role in that world. Here is a list of those questions:

- Where did we come from? How did the universe come to exist?

- Is there a God, and what relationship does that God have with the universe?

- Why are we here? Is there a purpose for humankind?

- What is the reason we are here, and more specifically, why am I here? Is there a purpose for my living in the world?

- What does it mean to live well, and what is the wisest way to do so? Is there some kind of ultimate good I should be living for?

- Where do we go when we die? Is this world all there is – do heaven and hell (or any other place exist), and what gets you to one or the other?

- Of all the concerns I have, what should be my ultimate concern, and how should I live in light of that concern?

Developing a Worldview:
Understanding How the World Works

Whether we are religious or philosophical (or not), these questions need to be addressed in the life of every person, if they truly intend to live well. When it comes to understanding our world and our place in it, we must render our own explanation of the world, of the possibility of a God and our knowing him/it/them, and our place in this short, challenging life. While we may act as if these questions do not matter, sooner or later every person must come to grips with them in their own lives. We all are in a search for ultimate meaning, the real meaning of life. We can rely on society, or culture, or family to give us the answers, but, sooner or later, we must adopt *our own* vision of things, *our* story, and live by it, through it, and within it. For us at least, that story will be what we count to be true, right, and good. If we are wrong in our choice of what the world truly means, we might be in danger of having wasted our entire lives on things that don't really matter at all.

Worldview = The Stories We Tell Ourselves to Make Sense of Our Lives

In the last chapter I provided an overview of the role that God's story should play in the life of a follower of Christ. I have always loved stories, been shaped by stories, and have sought to learn the craft of telling good stories. Dr. Leland Ryken, one of my professors from Wheaton College, shared passionately and persuasively with us on the richness of story in literature, film, and the arts. In stories we come to see the centrality and complexity of human experience, the richness of human affections, and the use of our imaginations (i.e., our ability to create and live in worlds made plain in the stories we tell). In human fictional stories we come to see and feel the power of concrete image, action, and symbol, the ability to enter into new spaces of heightened reality, and the joy of seeing the artistic craftsmanship of a story well told.

William J. Bausch lists ten propositions related to story theology that help us understand the significance and importance of the study of stories and the understanding of Bible and theology.[8]

1. Stories introduce us to *sacramental presences.*

2. Stories are always more important than *facts.*

3. Stories remain *normative (authoritative)* for the Christian community of faith.

4. *Christian traditions* evolve and define themselves through and around stories.

5. The stories of God precede, produce, and empower *the community of God's people.*

6. Community story implies *censure, rebuke, and accountability.*

7. Stories produce *theology.*

8. Stories produce *many theologies.*

9. Stories produce *ritual and sacrament.*

10. Stories are *history.*

Bausch, a wonderful teller of both biblical and folk tales, through these propositions offers an insightful look into the relationship of story to theology and history. As disciples of the Story of God, we need to always seek to be clear on the role of the Kingdom to the biblical narrative, and how that relates to our new identity in Christ.

Reversal and the Biblical Framework of the Kingdom

Every great story has a center, a core, a unifying motif, theme, or idea that provides harmony, connection, and integration to every character, episode, and scene in the story. One of the most important theological concepts associated with the rule of God (i.e., the Kingdom) in Scripture is the principle of *reversal.*[9] The story of the Kingdom (which is historical and true) as outlined in the Scriptures concerns God's intent to reverse the effects of Satan's rebellion, the disobedience of the first human pair, and the lasting impact their fall has had on creation: the curse, death, sin, and judgment.

Without a doubt, the Kingdom of God is God's sovereign intent to re-establish his rule and authority in this world, and to do so through the redemptive work of his Son, Jesus of Nazareth. This effort to "make things new" again is the core biblical teaching of Jesus and the ultimate point of reference on the meaning of life, under God's rule. The Kingdom Story was the heart of Jesus's teaching, and is the central focus of biblical theology. The values and moral vision of the Kingdom Story are final criterion for judging truth and value, and are an indispensable key to understanding human history.

It is not the intent of this chapter to explore the wide ranging implications of this reversal inherent in God's actions in Christ, but to limit the discussion to the main core of the argument: how does our understanding of reversal train us to better live into the meaning of the Kingdom in our lives and identities as agents and ambassadors of Christ. For a fuller discussion of the broader meaning of the Kingdom, I refer the reader to the works of George Eldon Ladd, whose writings outline in great detail the biblical and theological nuances of the Kingdom, and God's efforts to restore the universe under his reign.

The Already/Not Yet Kingdom

In assessing Jesus's unique teaching about the Kingdom over against his contemporaries, one of the prime distinctives is Jesus's claim that with his appearance in the world the Kingdom (at least in part) *had appeared and had drawn near at hand* (Mark 1.14-15 – Now after John was arrested, Jesus came into Galilee, proclaiming the gospel of God, [15] and saying, "The time is fulfilled, and the kingdom of God is at hand; repent and believe in the gospel.")

The Old Testament promise was clear: God almighty had promised the first human pair that he would send an anointed one, the Messiah, to come and offer his life as a sacrifice for sin, reveal the Father's glory to the nations, and restore the world and creation under God's reign. The effects of the curse and death would be overcome, and the failure of Adam's transgression and Israel's disobedience would be "recapitulated" – the Messiah would succeed where they had failed in representing the interests and reign of God. And, in the end, the "strong man" (i.e., Satan) who illegitimately held captive humankind would be judged, destroyed, and overcome through the Messiah's righteousness and power. We who believe know this Messiah to be none other than Jesus of Nazareth, the Son of God, who gave his life for the world (John 1.14-18; 3.16-18; 3.36; 10.16-18; 11.23-34, etc.).

With the coming of Jesus into the world through the virgin Mary and the conception of the Holy Spirit (theologically called the incarnation), the life of the Age to Come was manifested in a newer, fuller way than at any time in the past. Of course, the reversal of God's Kingdom had salient moments of manifestation – the Exodus from Egypt, the entering into the Promised Land, the destruction and captivity of Israel and Judah, and the return of the remnant back to the Land. These notable acts of God demonstrated God's ability to reverse the conditions of those lost, broken, and oppressed, and to rescue them, establishing a people under his reign. The incarnation, however, is a unique and final act of reversal, where the power and glory of God are manifest in his Son, a full living manifestation of the inauguration of the Age to Come into this present age. The uniqueness and finality of God's revelation in Christ is seen in the prologue of the book of Hebrews:

> Long ago, at many times and in many ways, God spoke to our fathers by the prophets, [2] but in these last days he has spoken to us by his Son, whom he appointed the heir of all things, through whom also he created the world. [3] He is the radiance of the glory of God and the exact imprint of his nature, and he upholds the universe by the word of his power. After making purification for sins, he sat down at the right hand of the Majesty on high, [4] having become as much superior to angels as the name he has inherited is more excellent than theirs.
>
> ~ Hebrews 1.1-4

Of all the "many times and many ways" God revealed his glory and word to the prophets of his intent to restore creation, the final and distinctive way in this age was the revelation given through his Son. In every respect the coming of Jesus is the coming of the Kingdom's presence in this world. The preaching and ministry of John the Baptist corresponds to the ministry of Elijah who would declare the coming of Messiah (Matt. 11.2-6). The inauguration of Jesus's ministry at Nazareth begins with his quotation of Isaiah and the ministry of Messiah, which he said, was fulfilled in their hearing that Sabbath morning:

> And he came to Nazareth, where he had been brought up. And as was his custom, he went to the synagogue on the Sabbath day, and he stood up to read. [17] And the scroll of the prophet Isaiah was given to him. He unrolled the scroll and found the place where it was written, [18] "The Spirit of the Lord is upon me, because he has anointed me to proclaim good news to the poor. He has sent me to proclaim liberty to the captives and recovering of sight to the blind, to set at liberty those who are oppressed, [19] to proclaim the year of the Lord's favor." [20] And he rolled up the scroll and gave it back to the attendant and sat down. And the eyes of all in the synagogue were fixed on him. [21] And he began to say to them, "Today this Scripture has been fulfilled in your hearing."
>
> ~ Luke 4.16-21

All of Jesus's acts – including his miracles, exorcisms, teaching, healings, and his person – gave a clear sign that the Kingdom had come in part through his incarnation. The reversal of God's Kingdom was on full display! Jesus's exorcisms and confrontations with demonic forces revealed that God was reestablishing his rule among humankind (e.g., Luke 10.18ff.; 11.20), and his teaching and claim of absolute authority on earth confessed God's intent to restore his rule under Christ, visible for all to see (cf. Mark 2.1-12; Matt. 21.27; 28.18). The "strong man" ravishing

humankind has now been bound (Matt. 12.28-29). Jesus's entrance
into the world constitutes the invasion and manifestation of
God's kingly power and authority into the world.

> Knowing their thoughts, he said to them, "Every kingdom
> divided against itself is laid waste, and no city or house divided
> against itself will stand. [26] And if Satan casts out Satan, he is
> divided against himself. How then will his kingdom stand? [27]
> And if I cast out demons by Beelzebul, by whom do your sons
> cast them out? Therefore they will be your judges. [28] But if it is
> by the Spirit of God that I cast out demons, then the kingdom
> of God has come upon you. [29] Or how can someone enter a
> strong man's house and plunder his goods, unless he first binds
> the strong man? Then indeed he may plunder his house. [30]
> Whoever is not with me is against me, and whoever does not
> gather with me scatters."
>
> ~ Matthew 12.25-30

Reversal and the Two Advents of Christ
According to both Oscar Cullman (*Christ and Time*) and George
Ladd (*The Gospel of the Kingdom* and *The Presence of the Future*)
the Kingdom of God (God's rule and reign restored in creation)
occurs in two distinct displays or manifestations (advents), both
associated with comings of the Son of God into the world. In
the first advent of Jesus into the world, the rebellious prince was
bound, his house looted, and the penalty for humankind was
paid on the Cross, and vindicated through the resurrection and
establishment of the Church. This is the "Already" side of the
"Already/Not Yet" Kingdom.

In the second advent of Christ (which is yet to come) the rebellious
prince will be finally destroyed, the effects of the curse and death
will be finally overcome, and the beauty and grace of God's
kingdom rule will be manifested fully, when Jesus comes and

restores all things under God's rule in a new heaven and earth. This represents the "Not Yet" side of the "Already/Not Yet" Kingdom.

This understanding of the Kingdom helps us make sense of the life and mission of Jesus *during his incarnation*, as well as the consummation of his work *at the Second Coming*. In the incarnation, his *mission* was to destroy the works of the devil (1 John 3.8), and his *birth* represents the invasion of God into Satan's dominion (Luke 1.31-33). Jesus's *message* was the Kingdom's proclamation and inauguration (Mark 1.14-15), and his *teaching* outlined the ethics of the Kingdom (Matt. 5-7). His *miracles* were demonstrations of his kingly authority and power (Mark 2.8-12), and his *exorcisms* revealed his defeat of the power of the devil and his angels (Luke 11.14-20). His *life and deeds* reveal the glory of the Father and the majesty of the Kingdom (John 1.14-18).

His *death* represents the sacrifice for sin and cosmic deliverance of the Kingdom's victory over death and the curse (Col. 2.15; Heb. 10.10-14). His *resurrection* both verifies his messiahship, and guarantees the victory of his redemptive work (Rom. 1.1-4). His *Great Commission* is his exalted call for his people to proclaim his kingdom victory to all the world (Matt. 28.18-20), and his *ascension* represents his coronation as King and Lord over all (Eph. 1.15-23; Heb. 1.2-4). The *coming of his Holy Spirit at Pentecost* was the pledge and "down payment" (*arrabon*) of the full promise of the Kingdom (2 Cor. 1.20), and the *formation of the church* there represents the community and foretaste of the Kingdom's life in this world (2 Cor. 5.18-21). His *session in heaven* as risen Lord represents his generalship of God's church in the earth (1 Cor. 15.24-28), and his *Second Coming* will be the final consummation of the Kingdom (Rev. 19-22).

What do all these theological claims mean for you and me? These biblical affirmations prove that God almighty has determined from eternity past to reverse the effects of the curse (death, disease, war, alienation, despair, and bondage) in this world. God is on the move. Put simply: God's rule is in effect. God can do anything with anyone in any place to fulfill his purpose and establish his Kingdom. Even though it appears that the devil, evil, sin, and death are winning, they cannot prevail. Even though the "check engine" light has been on in the universe for millennia, with the coming of Christ in the world God almighty is reversing the impact of Satan and the curse, and restoring all things under his rule again. He is disarming the powers of evil and abolishing death in our midst today through his Son, Jesus Christ. These and other texts affirm this truth:

> He disarmed the rulers and authorities and put them to open shame, by triumphing over them in him.
>
> ~ Colossians 2.15

> Since therefore the children share in flesh and blood, he himself likewise partook of the same things, that through death he might destroy the one who has the power of death, that is, the devil.
>
> ~ Hebrews 2.14

> Therefore do not be ashamed of the testimony about our Lord, nor of me his prisoner, but share in suffering for the gospel by the power of God, [9] who saved us and called us to a holy calling, not because of our works but because of his own purpose and grace, which he gave us in Christ Jesus before the ages began, [10] and which now has been manifested through the appearing of our Savior Christ Jesus, who abolished death and brought life and immortality to light through the gospel.
>
> ~ 2 Timothy 1.8-10

Unlikely Places, Unlovely People, Unimaginable Purposes

Practically speaking, understanding the principle of reversal means that things are simply not what they seem. However defeated, messed up, or dubious things might appear, the power of the Kingdom of God can reverse it. God can do the unexpected with the most questionable folk. The grace of God is in full effect. God can transform and rescue even the most horrible circumstance, the most absurd person, or the weirdest condition and turn it around (like a U-turn) for the purposes of his Kingdom's advance.

Take for instance unlikely places. What are the odds that the Messiah and Lord of the universe would grow up, in all places, Nazareth of Galilee?

> The next day Jesus decided to go to Galilee. He found Philip and said to him, "Follow me." [44] Now Philip was from Bethsaida, the city of Andrew and Peter. [45] Philip found Nathanael and said to him, "We have found him of whom Moses in the Law and also the prophets wrote, Jesus of Nazareth, the son of Joseph." [46] Nathanael said to him, "Can anything good come out of Nazareth?" Philip said to him, "Come and see."
>
> ~ John 1.43-46

Only the Gospels and Acts use the term *Nazarene* or *Nazareth* in the New Testament. It was an insignificant place at the time of Jesus, both in terms of size and population, probably around sixty acres able to support a few people under five hundred. Only one citation in the New Testament appears to be a *positive one* (Matt. 2.23), which cites a kind of phantom text in the Old Testament. Historically, Nazareth was associated with dubious and unimpressive characters (see Hiram's reaction to Solomon's gift of some of the cities of Galilee to him, 1 Kings 9.11-13). In the book of Acts, Nazareth was associated with sectarian and cultic behavior as seen in Tertullus' oratory before Felix in Acts 24.4-5:

> But, to detain you no further, I beg you in your kindness to hear us briefly. [5] For we have found this man a plague, one who stirs up riots among all the Jews throughout the world and is a ringleader of the sect of the Nazarenes.
>
> ~ Acts 24.4-5

Add to this, the historical references by Tertullian who cites that Jews used Nazarene as an anti-Christian slur, as did Muslims and Persians, and emperor Julian[10] who used "Nazarenes" and "Galilean" as anti-civil descriptions of weird folk. God *chose* to raise his Son, the victor over evils, in *Nazareth*. He can raise anyone from anywhere to do anything he wishes to do. Because of reversal, we need never judge a person by where they are from, or what their history or background is. God is reversing the trends and odds for every person who believes, regardless of their past or place of origin. Because he is Lord, we all can be free!

What about *unlovely people*? No one who spends time in the Kingdom Story can avoid the unsavory cast of characters that make up the historical narrative of God's kingdom rescue. The patriarchs all had moral blind spots: Abraham was a liar, Isaac was clueless, and Jacob was a schemer. Moses was a murderer and a fugitive, Rahab was a prostitute, and Samson was a showboat. David was an adulterer and murderer, and Jonah abandoned his post. God's people (in both Israel and Judah) were idolaters, and slow-responders to God's will. What a cast of characters!

Frankly, the New Testament is no different. Zaccheus was an embezzler, Matthew, the publican, was a traitor, Mary Magdalene had issues with demonic oppression, and Peter was a betrayer. What of you and I: are we not the fickle and the forlorn?

What this small list representing the folk in Jesus's storyline reveals is that the background, pedigree, or moral history of a person says nothing of what God almighty can do with someone, literally *anyone* he chooses to call, transform, and release to do his will. He is the God of the impossible and the implausible!

We should be very careful before we begin to quote statistical data on the odds of people being different than they are. Actually, no one can enter the Kingdom of God unless they are born again, born of the Spirit and of God (John 3.3-6). Pretending that you are okay because you have not committed any egregious (*really bad*) sins doesn't make you righteous. Nor does being willing to consign somebody to the "dark side" because of where they've been or what they've done in anti-kingdom and grace. God can do anything with anyone in any place to fulfill his kingdom will. He selects whom he will to accomplish what he wants–and nobody gets to veto his choice!

Finally, what of *unimaginable purposes*? The principle of reversal in the Lord's Kingdom suggests that our God has chosen to operate on a plain and level different than the one on which the world operates. He has a penchant for broken things, for little ragged people, for causes against all odds, for impossible dreams. The good theology of the historically Black church put it this way: "God can make a way out of no way." God's thoughts and ways are not our thoughts and ways (Isa. 55.8-11), and he enjoys to select those on the bottom and to exalt them to the top. God has deliberately chosen the poor and the broken and the small to accomplish his kingdom purposes!

Listen, my beloved brothers, has not God chosen those who are poor in the world to be rich in faith and heirs of the kingdom, which he has promised to those who love him?

~ James 2.5

For consider your calling, brothers: not many of you were wise according to worldly standards, not many were powerful, not many were of noble birth. [27] But God chose what is foolish in the world to shame the wise; God chose what is weak in the world to shame the strong; [28] God chose what is low and despised in the world, even things that are not, to bring to nothing things that are, [29] so that no human being might boast in the presence of God.

~ 1 Corinthians 1.26-29

He has shown strength with his arm; he has scattered the proud in the thoughts of their hearts; [52] he has brought down the mighty from their thrones and exalted those of humble estate; [53] he has filled the hungry with good things, and the rich he has sent away empty.

~ Luke 1.51-53

The Ethics of Reversal:
The Values of the Upside-Down Kingdom

One of my favorite studies over the years has been to collect and meditate upon the explicit statements of reversal that are mentioned in the NT, most of which were mentioned by Christ, but also the other apostles. What this list reveals is that the heartbeat and pulse of the Kingdom is this turning-everything-upside-down nature of God's rule. Look at how reversal shapes and informs everything God does in a world where righteousness and justice are rarely seen and practiced:

- The poor shall become rich, and the rich shall become poor, Luke 6.20-26.

- The law breaker and the undeserving are saved, Matt. 21.31-32.

- Those who humble themselves shall be exalted, 1 Pet. 5.5-6.

- Those who exalt themselves shall be brought low, Luke 18.14.

- The blind shall be given sight, John 9.39.

- Those claiming to see shall be made blind, John 9.40-41.

- We only become truly free by being Christ's slave, Rom. 12.1-2.

- God has chosen what is foolish to shame the wise, 1 Cor. 1.27.

- God has chosen what is weak in the world to shame the strong, 1 Cor. 1.27.

- God has chosen the low and despised to bring to nothing things that are, 1 Cor. 1.28.

- We only gain the next world by losing and letting go of this one, 1 Tim. 6.7.

- Love this life and you'll lose it; hate this life, and you'll keep the next John 12.25.

- You become the greatest by being the servant of all, Mark 10.42-45.

- Store up treasures here, and you forfeit heaven's reward, Matt. 6.19.

- Store up treasures above in order to gain heaven's wealth, Matt. 6.20.

- Only if you truly die to yourself can you fully come to live again, John 12.24.

- Release all earthly reputation to gain heaven's favor, Phil. 3.3-7.

- The first shall be last, and the last shall become first, Mark 9.35.

- The grace of Jesus is perfected in your weakness, not in your strength, 2 Cor. 12.9.

- God's highest sacrifice is contrition and brokenness, Ps.51.17.

- It is better to give to others than to receive from them, Acts 20.35.

- Give away all you have in order to obtain God's best, Luke 6.38.

Conclusion

When you look at the Story of God and fly-over kingdom truth, you begin to see how God is reversing the effects of sin and Satan to reestablish God's sovereign purpose in the world. The petition of the Lord's prayer is the heart cry of the universe: "Your kingdom come, your will be done, on earth as it is in heaven" (Matt. 6.10). God does whatever he pleases (Ps. 135.6), and his counsels and plans stand forever, to all generations (Ps. 33.11; 115.3). If we intend to live the way God sees things, to really get our pretense on, we will need to see God as the central actor in the unfolding drama of life. He is on a mission to recover everything that was lost at the beginning of time.

The issue is not God's plan for your life; rather, it has always been "will you fulfill your part in the great plan of God to reverse the rebellion of Satan's infernal rebellion and humankind's tragic fall?" God is reversing all things to the way they are supposed to be. Accept your call to get your pretense on, embrace the risen Lord as King, and join God's great adventure of reversal by laying it all down for Christ and his Kingdom.

In the next chapter, we will explore the role the Church plays in the telling of God's Story, and the advance of his Kingdom of reversal – and the part you are meant to play within it.

CHAPTER 3

"There's Plenty Good Room": The Centrality of the Church in God's Kingdom Advance

> And I tell you, you are Peter, and on this rock I will build my church, and the gates of hell shall not prevail against it.
>
> ~ Matthew 16.18

When I was a young boy, I used to love to go to church with my family. It was an amazing experience for me – all the sights, sounds, and sympathies of a poor black congregation left an indelible imprint on the consciousness of a little kid like me. I can remember seeing grown people weep and march and moan and sing. I still remember Mr. Foster, the official prayer warrior of our congregation, a rotund, deep-voiced, gentle man whom the pastor would call forward to the altar, who will echo in our little room supplications in Jesus's name for the small yet zealous assembly. I remember Miss Jenkins on the piano, a tall slender lady with musical genius, who played the piano like a Motown Liberace and couldn't read a note of sheet music. I still can hear in my memory the eight-member choir whose "pipes" were so robust they could blow your hair back, even if you were sitting in the nether regions of that little church house. Amazing services, lasting most of the day, all amazing, all different, all anointed.

One of the songs our little church sang was a rousing chorus to welcome newly repented sinners into our fold, or to make pleas to those who were on the boundaries of salvation, anxiously deciding whether to join our happy few or not. The song was called *Plenty Good Room*, and the chorus said this:

> There's plenty good room, plenty good room, plenty good room in my Father's Kingdom, yes, there's plenty good room, plenty good room – choose your seat, and sit down!

These simple words were sung over and over and over again, while the preacher made his impassioned pleas to those in attendance to hear the voice of Jesus calling to them, quit fighting his invitation, and come into the fold of salvation and grace. He would beg, and exhort, and cheer, and call out, always ensuring the audience that the Kingdom of God was never full, that there was plenty good room for him or her in the church, and all they needed to do is to respond with faith to God's call. They simply needed to "choose their seat, and sit down!"

That little church was everything to us – our recreation center, our educational wing, our party place, and our spiritual retreat home. Filled with small people all of whom were black, it was an island of inspiration in a world of rejection, oppression, and injustice. None of them were able to vote or participate in the body politic, few of them had ever had access to higher education, nearly all of them raised their families with great difficulty economically, supported by low paying, manual labor jobs. Like Paul said to the Corinthians in his first epistle "For consider your calling, brothers: not many of you were wise according to worldly standards, not many were powerful, not many were of noble birth" (1 Cor. 1.26). They were porters, trash haulers, meat packers, painters, handymen and women, maids, cooks, barely scratching by at a time when it was difficult to be Black in America.

Still, the one place on this earth that respected them, nourished them, where they were full partners in kingdom life and ministry, was that little assembly, Grant Chapel African Methodist Episcopal Church. Black America-remixed Anglicans in inner city Wichita, Kansas! What a sight, and what a wonder! An embassy of the Most High God – in the ghetto community of Negro poor folk. God does work in mysterious ways, doesn't he, his wonders to perform?

I want to talk about the centrality of the church in forming our identity and understanding of God's will for our lives today. Admittedly, things have dramatically changed since our family gathered in the little chapel property on Piatt Street in inner-city Wichita. On the surface, by all accounts, it would appear that the church is either in a holding pattern, or worse, in significant retreat. The church and its leaders tend to hold less and less authority in the affairs of our western society, and specifically in American society. The Hartford Institute for Religion Research's figures reveals a church in wholesale retreat:

- 600,000 clergy (pastors, retired clergy, chaplains, ordained faculty), and 335,000 congregations in North America
- 1,400 leave the ministry each month (a burgeoning shortage of dire proportions)
- 50,000 attendees leave the Church weekly (disillusioned American church-goers)
- At least 4,000 churches die each year

Grant Chapel A. M. E. Church was an outpost of the Kingdom of God for the poor, working class "Negroes" who attended it faithfully, sounding forth the Gospel in a community oppressed from the outside and ravaged by poverty and nihilism from within. It is hard to comprehend what our lives would have been like without our mother, our strength, and our home, the local church. The pastor was not only the spiritual leader of our congregation, but the point person for our social lives, our advocate in all issues of well being, and family, and life. Contrast this role with how the local church is faring in the lives of many Christ followers today.

I cannot express how shocked I was to read the noted George Barna's reflection of the role of the local church in our spiritual journeys today. Here is an extended quote from his book *Revolution*, written (I think) to provide new clarity of the role of the church in the community and the world:

> The point here is simply to recognize that if we place all our hope in the local church, it is a misplaced hope. Many well-intentioned pastors promote this perspective by proclaiming, "The local church is the hope of the world." Like most advertising slogans, this notion is emotionally appealing. The trouble is, the sentiment is not biblical. Jesus, and Jesus alone, is the hope of the world. The local church is one mechanism that can be instrumental in bringing us closer to Him and helping us to be more like Him. But, as the research data clearly shows, churches are not doing the job. If the local church is the hope of the world, then the world has no hope.

> There is nothing inherently wrong with being involved in a local church. But realize that being part of a group that calls itself a "church" does not make you saved, holy, righteous, or godly any more than being in Yankee Stadium makes you a professional baseball player. Participating in church-based activities does not necessarily draw you closer to God or prepare you for a life that satisfies Him or enhances your existence. Being a member of a congregation does not make you spiritually righteous any more

than being a member of the Democratic Party makes you a liberal wing nut.

Being in a right relationship with God and His people is what matters. Scripture teaches us that devoting your life to loving God with all your heart, mind, strength, and soul is what honors Him. Being part of a local church may facilitate that. Or it might not.[11]

I believe we cannot get our pretense on truly without a revival of our understanding of the centrality of the church in God's kingdom work, and the implications of that in our every day lives. Only if we understand and embrace the centrality of the church in God's sovereign purpose can we truly live out our true role in his great Story of the Kingdom of God today.

The Church Is Central in God's Sovereign Purpose to Redeem His Creation

Even a cursory reading of the Bible reveals God's determination to save a people for himself out of the fallen human race. The voluntary rebellion of Adam and Eve, the first human pair, did not result in God's final rejection of humanity. Rather, through God's promise to them in the Garden of Eden, the Lord assured them he would send a glorious conqueror who would crush the skull (up-end the reign and dominion) of the serpent who caused our first parents to fall. "I will put enmity between you and the woman, and between your offspring and her offspring; he shall bruise your head, and you shall bruise his heel" (Gen. 3.15).

This divine promise to bring into the world that "offspring of the woman" in many ways constitutes the center of God's cosmic drama, and the story of salvation narrated so carefully in the pages of Scripture. From the garden to Noah to the Tower of

Babel, and then to the patriarchs, the Bible outlines God's sovereign determination to rescue humankind from its own worst rebellion through a Savior who would come through the lineage of Abram, later to be named Abraham. "Now the Lord said to Abram, 'Go from your country and your kindred and your father's house to the land that I will show you. And I will make of you a great nation, and I will bless you and make your name great, so that you will be a blessing. I will bless those who bless you, and him who dishonors you I will curse, and in you all the families of the earth shall be blessed'" (Gen. 12.1-3). Notice the contours of God's covenant promise to Abraham given here:

- I will make of you a "great nation"
- I will bless you and make your name great
- So that you will be a blessing
- I will bless those who bless, curse those who curse
- By you all the families of the earth shall be blessed (bless themselves)

Essentially, the story of God outlined in Scripture can be conveniently divided into two, dramatically unequal parts. Part 1 is Genesis 1.1-3.15; Part 2 is Genesis 3.15 - Revelation 22.21! Genesis 3.15 represents the dividing line of the Bible's overall theme; God is a warrior who is fighting in divine conflict with holy resolve to redeem creation from the power of the curse. "Whoever makes a practice of sinning is of the devil, for the devil has been sinning from the beginning. The reason the Son of God appeared was to destroy the works of the devil" (1 John 3.8). The purpose of the Incarnation of Jesus Christ was to destroy the works of Satan, the original rebellion which led to the corruption and bondage of this present age.

This promise-fulfillment rhythm is the primary guiding motif of Scripture, and it underwrites all truly sound biblical exegetical theology. We get a clue to this structure in the genealogy of Matthew's Gospel, which essentially records Christ's origins from Adam to Abraham, from Abraham to David, and finally from David to Christ (Matt. 1.1). God's intent in his sacred covenant, announced in the garden and fortified with the patriarchs and the nation, was to make Jesus Christ the center of all the universe, and through him, to bring together a people who would belong to him for all eternity, which, amazingly, included us, the Gentiles.

This amazing unfolding biblical drama is not merely a story of a provincial people with a tribal deity who fights for the descendants of Abraham, the people of Israel alone. Rather, the biblical story is a story of God's election of his people Israel who were designed to serve as the people through whom God's anointed King would come. This special Elect of God, the Messiah, would reveal the Father's glory to us, redeem us from the Curse, and restore the world, under God's reign. This notion of Israel as the nation through whom he would come for the saving of humankind was a notion either unknown or unaccepted by God's people Israel. The Scriptures declare, however, that God's determination from the beginning was to bring together a new people, of both Jews and Gentiles, into existence which would shine forth his praise together, as a new humanity under his kingdom reign.

Three key NT texts suggest that the Church and its inclusion of non-Jewish peoples, the Gentiles, represents the very heart of the revelation of God's mystery (cf. Rom. 16.25-27; Eph. 3.7-10, and Col. 1.25-27). Here are those three texts below, so you can see the argument Paul makes about the mystery in his epistles.

> Now to him who is able to strengthen you according to my gospel and the preaching of Jesus Christ, according to the

revelation of the mystery that was kept secret for long ages [26] but has now been disclosed and through the prophetic writings *has been made known to all nations*, according to the command of the eternal God, to bring about the obedience of faith – [27] to the only wise God be glory forevermore through Jesus Christ! Amen.

~ Romans 16.25-27

Of this gospel I was made a minister according to the gift of God's grace, which was given me by the working of his power. [8] To me, though I am the very least of all the saints, this grace was given, *to preach to the Gentiles the unsearchable riches of Christ*, [9] and to bring to light for everyone what is the plan of the mystery hidden for ages in God who created all things, [10] so that through the church the manifold wisdom of God might now be made known to the rulers and authorities in the heavenly places.

~ Ephesians 3.7-10

. . . of which I became a minister according to the stewardship from God that was given to me for you, to make the word of God fully known, [26] the mystery hidden for ages and generations but now revealed to his saints. [27] *To them God chose to make known how great among the Gentiles are the riches of the glory of this mystery*, which is Christ in you, the hope of glory [italics mine].

~ Colossians 1.25-27

In each of these texts we see the wonder and disclosure of God's inclusion of the peoples of the world in his sovereign purpose and plan for salvation (e.g., Gal. 3.7-9 – "Know then that it is those of faith who are the sons of Abraham. [8] And the Scripture, foreseeing that God would justify the Gentiles by faith, preached the gospel beforehand to Abraham, saying, 'In you shall all the nations be blessed.' [9] So then, those who are of faith are blessed along with Abraham, the man of faith.") Indeed, the life and light of Jesus Christ penetrated our darkness, and now, through his incarnation, death, and resurrection, we Gentiles have seen a great light (Isa. 9.1-2).

So then, we who believe in the Gospel together, both Jew and Gentile, are the new family of God (1 John 3.1-3), the body of Christ (Rom. 12.4-5), and the temple of the Holy Spirit (1 Cor. 3.16). We are the new dwelling place of God, built on the foundation of the prophets and the apostles, with Christ himself being the cornerstone, fitted together through the work of the Holy Spirit (Eph. 2.19-22). Every little, homely assembly where Jesus is confessed as Lord, where the Gospel is preached, the repentant are baptized, where the sacraments are administered, and the discipline of the church enjoyed – *each one of these congregations* (a *local* church) is a true instance of the one, holy, apostolic, and catholic (universal) church of the living God. The church is central for in us God reveals his determination to redeem his creation from the power of the curse, and draw out of humankind a people for himself forever (Ps. 22.26-27). As a believer in Christ, you are a member of God's forever family; you are an heir of the coming Kingdom of our Lord!

The Church Is Central in Comprehending God's Heart for All Humankind

As stated in the earlier part of this work, God almighty has been working from the start to redeem a new humankind from the Curse, Death, and the effects of the Fall. He intends to accomplish this through his Son, identifying all whom he saves with the person of Jesus Christ.

Indeed, at the very heart of the universe lies a marvelous cosmic drama, authored by our triune God himself, which is nothing less than a divine romance, a marvelous and epic true myth and legend of an undying love relationship between an Almighty

God, and a people. Don't be shocked by words and phrases like "cosmic drama," "divine romance," or "myth and legend." I agree with both J. R. R. Tolkien and C. S. Lewis that say essentially the Christian story is "true myth," the "tale of all tales," the one story which gives clarity and unifies all true depictions of who we are and where we are going. To be Christian is to be authentic participants and living witnesses of this story; we literally have been chosen to live out our parts in God's cosmic story. This is the essence of "getting our pretense on;" we are called to play our own unique roles in the drama of the ages.

The Scriptures refer to God's story with his people in various metaphors and figures, including that of a mighty warrior rescuing his people, a divine shepherd bringing his fold together, or a King restoring his reign after the rebellion of his peoples. One of the most illuminating figures is that of the romance of God with his people. This notion of God wooing his people from lostness to be his bride is clearly illustrated throughout the Scriptures, between God and his people Israel, and the Lord and his Church (e.g., Isa. 62.5; Song of Sol.; Ezek. 16.8-16). Here are a few examples of God using this metaphor to describe his love for his people:

> I will greatly rejoice in the Lord; my soul shall exult in my God, for he has clothed me with the garments of salvation; he has covered me with the robe of righteousness, as a bridegroom decks himself like a priest with a beautiful headdress, and as a bride adorns herself with her jewels.
>
> ~ Isaiah 61.10

> For as a young man marries a young woman, so shall your sons marry you, and as the bridegroom rejoices over the bride, so shall your God rejoice over you.
>
> ~ Isaiah 62.5

Let us rejoice and exult and give him the glory, for the marriage of the Lamb has come, and his Bride has made herself ready; [8] it was granted her to clothe herself with fine linen, bright and pure" – for the fine linen is the righteous deeds of the saints.

~ Revelation 19.7-8

These texts illustrate this central biblical motif, one which you as a Christian should embrace and live into. You see, God describes his rescue as a tale of divine romance and passion for his people. If you think going to church is a little deal with no meaning, mostly boring, and easily ignored, you need to ponder these truths afresh. This romance and passion is God's most deep burden, clearly seen in the drama of Christ and the Church, with Christ as the Bridegroom and the Church as his bride (Matt. 9.15; 25.1ff.; John 3.29; Rev. 21.2). John the Baptizer understood his ministry for and relationship to Jesus in this way ("The one who has the bride is the bridegroom. The friend of the bridegroom, who stands and hears him, rejoices greatly at the bridegroom's voice. Therefore this joy of mine is now complete", John 3.29.)

You also see how Paul integrated his communication with the believers of his day with this clear understanding of Christ's relationship to his people, the church. For instance, when he exhorted the believing husbands to high moral treatment in their conduct with their spouses, he referred to Christ's relationship with his people:

Husbands, love your wives, as Christ loved the church and gave himself up for her, [26] that he might sanctify her, having cleansed her by the washing of water with the word, [27] so that he might present the church to himself in splendor, without spot or wrinkle or any such thing, that she might be holy and without blemish.

~ Ephesians 5.25-27

John the apostle, in his vision of the end, referred to our final destination, the holy city, the New Jerusalem, as being dressed in the attire of a bride to be given to her husband (Rev. 21.2 – And I saw the holy city, new Jerusalem, coming down out of heaven from God, prepared as a bride adorned for her husband.) This relationship is referred to through the Bible as the end of God's divine rescue of a new people for himself – a bride being prepared to be his and his alone, forever.

This bridegroom-bride relationship rightly defines the goal of all apostolic ministry – to present the church to Christ as a "chaste virgin" (2 Cor. 11.2 – I feel a divine jealousy for you, for I betrothed you to one husband, to present you as a pure virgin to Christ.) Paul viewed his role as one who was charged with presenting the church to Christ as a bride prepared for her husband. In my judgment, this is the way to view and read Jesus's reply to Peter's confession, his notion of "building his church":

> He said to them, "But who do you say that I am?" [16] Simon Peter replied, "You are the Christ, the Son of the living God." [17] And Jesus answered him, "Blessed are you, Simon Bar-Jonah! For flesh and blood has not revealed this to you, but my Father who is in heaven. [18] And I tell you, you are Peter, and on this rock I will build my church, and the gates of hell shall not prevail against it. [19] I will give you the keys of the kingdom of heaven, and whatever you bind on earth shall be bound in heaven, and whatever you loose on earth shall be loosed in heaven."
>
> ~ Matthew 16.15-19

Viewed in this way, the church (universal and every Jesus-honoring local assembly) is central in God's dealings with human affairs through this figure of the bride. God's passion is to draw out a remnant of humankind for his own possession, those with whom he will dwell forever in a new heavens and earth. His Son is redeeming from all nations this one, holy bride made up of every boy, girl, woman and man from every age and place who have acknowledged Jesus as Lord. The Spirit is drawing the peoples of the earth to Christ, for through him alone can any person be restored to right relationship with God. We are healed and adopted through him alone; there can be no authentic confession or practice of Christianity without incorporation into the person and body of Christ.

One of my favorite Latin Fathers of the Church is Cyprian, a third-century bishop whose teachings and homilies contributed greatly to communication of and clarity provided by our apostolic faith. In polished Latin, Cyprian, that great churchman and theologian, spoke eloquently of the essential nature of the Church to salvation and to Christ. For decades now I have summed up Cyprian's sentiment and the apostolic confession in this manner to my students: "If the church ain't yo' *mama*, then God ain't yo' *daddy*!"

This little statement sums up nicely the truth of this matter of the *organic* connection of Christ to the Church. To share in Christ is to share the same essential spiritual DNA that is shared by all believers in Christ, everywhere of every time, epoch, and age:

> Therefore go out from their midst, and be separate from them, says the Lord, and touch no unclean thing; then I will welcome you, [18] and I will be a father to you, and you shall be sons and daughters to me, says the Lord Almighty.
>
> ~ 2 Corinthians 6.17-18

> . . . for in Christ Jesus you are all sons of God, through faith.
>
> ~ Galatians 3.26

And because you are sons, God has sent the Spirit of his Son
into our hearts, crying, "Abba! Father!"

~ Galatians 4.6

See what kind of love the Father has given to us, that we should
be called children of God; and so we are. The reason why the
world does not know us is that it did not know him.

~ 1 John 3.1

And they sang a new song, saying, "Worthy are you to take the
scroll and to open its seals, for you were slain, and by your blood
you ransomed people for God from every tribe and language
and people and nation, [10] and you have made them a kingdom
and priests to our God, and they shall reign on the earth."

~ Revelation 5.9-10

These and other texts clearly establish the deep, spiritual
connection that each believer shares with all others, despite
race, background, culture, age, or place. And this connection
has numberless implications for the way in which we both
perceive and treat believers who are different from ourselves.
As I tell believers who are dramatically unlike myself, "*I am
the proverbial brother that your daddy never told you about!*"
In Christ, there is neither Greek nor Jew, circumcised nor
uncircumcised, Barbarian, sophisticated upper class folk, slave
or free person – in the church, Christ is all and in all (Col. 3.11).

Unfortunately today, many believers have a functional view of
church, that is, merely a place where you can be baptized, married,
or be given a nice memorial service, in other words, where you
are *hatched*, *matched*, and *dispatched*! And, to be perfectly honest,
many congregations are living with petty disputes, saturated in
the tiniest things while ignoring the weighty issues of the Kingdom.
As one commentator said: "The Church is like Noah's ark: if it
weren't for *the storm* outside you couldn't stand *the stink* inside!"

These kinds of views and issues must be rejected, if you are truly going to live into the truth of the church, who you really are, and get your pretense on regarding being one of God's elect bride members. Among all the other things you may be as a Christian, you must get your pretense on about being a member of the body of Christ. As amazing as it may sound, you have been chosen by God to live forever in a place that Christ has personally designed and built for you, and all those whom he claims as his own. In the timing of the Father's own plan, he will return and gather you and all others elected to be with him forever (John 14.1-3; 1 John 3.1-3; Titus 2.11-14). This is your identity and your destiny.

You Are "In Christ": A Member of the Body, Personally Identified with Christ

To get at this truly, you must begin to see that the church is identified completely with the Son of God, with the person and work of Christ. We are united with him, intimately and permanently. "Therefore a man shall leave his father and mother and hold fast to his wife, and the two shall become one flesh." This mystery is profound, and I am saying that it refers to Christ and the church" (Eph. 5.31-32).

The easiest way to illustrate this organic connection of Christ to his people in the church is to trace the apostolic claims of our being with him, in him, and through him in the New Testament. Here is a sampling of this critical confession of the apostles for us:

- We are *"made one in Christ,"* 1 Cor. 6.15-17.
- We were *baptized into him,* 1 Cor. 12.13.
- We *died with him,* Rom. 6.3-4.
- We were *buried with him,* Rom 6.3-4.
- We were *raised with him,* Eph. 2.4-7.

- We are *ascended with him*, Eph 2.6.
- We have been made to *sit with him in heavenly places*, Eph. 2.6.
- We have been called to *suffer with him*, Rom. 8.17-18.
- We will be caught up together *to him*, 1 Thess. 4.13-18.
- We will be *glorified with him*, Rom 8.17.
- We will be *resurrected in him*, 1Cor.15.48-49.
- We will be *made like him*, 1 John 3.2.
- We are *joint-heirs with him*, Rom. 8.17.
- We will *sit with him* on his throne and *reign forever with him*, Rev. 3.21.

What comes to your mind when you read that list of your intimate connection with Christ? You should be astounded, overwhelmed, amazed. Do you see that this connection occurs through your union with Christ and his people, that these are statements made of those whom he has redeemed and with whom he will share his glory? I would argue you cannot live into who you are as a Christian if you have a low, ignoble view of the church of Jesus Christ. Without her, there is no union with Christ, and no future in the Kingdom. And, the primary place where you can see the Church in action is the local assembly of believers. "We may be homely, but we are good!"

The Church Is Central in Kingdom Advance, Especially among the Poor

The Church is the locus and agent of the Kingdom, the enterprise that is responsible to proclaim and embody the transformation of the Kingdom. It is central in the transformation of the lives of the poor. God created the church for his own glory (Eph. 1.5-6), to share God's own nature (2 Pet. 1.3-4), and to challenge the dominion of Satan (Eph. 3.10-11). As the embodiment of Christ in the world, the Church is called to shine as lights in a dark place (1 Thess. 5.5-6; Phil. 2.15-16), to make disciples of all nations (Matt. 28.18-20; Acts 1.8), and to do good, exhibiting the righteousness and justice of the Kingdom wherever an assembly of Christ is planted (2 Cor. 5.18; Gal. 6.10; James 1.27; Rom. 13.12-14). The Church on the earth is to reflect the life and light of the Son of God in heaven (Matt. 5.13-16).

What is amazing about this high mission is the reversal intrinsic in her calling. God has chosen the poor of this world to be rich in faith, and heirs of the Kingdom. He has chosen those who are small, unimpressive, and unlovely to be the vehicle through which he will make known the life and light of the Kingdom. "Listen, my beloved brothers, has not God chosen those who are poor in the world to be rich in faith and heirs of the kingdom, which he has promised to those who love him?" (James 2.5). God has elected the small, the unimportant, the weak, the broken, and the neglected to do his bidding, to be the vessels of his kingdom life, and to general the forces of his kingdom advance. Contrary to what we may think, God has chosen the small in order that no one can boast in his presence.

> For consider your calling, brothers: not many of you were wise according to worldly standards, not many were powerful, not many were of noble birth. [27] But God chose what is foolish in the world to shame the wise; God chose what is weak in the world to shame the strong; [28] God chose what is low and despised in the world, even things that are not, to bring to nothing things that are, [29] so that no human being might boast in the presence of God. [30] And because of him you are in Christ Jesus, who became to us wisdom from God, righteousness and sanctification and redemption, [31] so that, as it is written, "Let the one who boasts, boast in the Lord."
>
> ~ 1 Corinthians 1.26-31

This election of the church as not worldly wise, not of noble birth, and generally those considered foolish, low and despised, and weak, is emblematic of the calling of the Messiah, whose marks and character corresponds to this selection of the lowly.

Consider Jesus's inaugural sermon at Nazareth, where he announced that he was anointed with the Spirit of the LORD to preach Good News to the poor (Luke 4.16-21). Think about how Jesus verified the confession and faith of Zacchaeus after he announced that half of his goods he would give to the poor, and restore fourfold those whom he had swindled (Luke 19.1-9). Think, too, of how our Lord throughout his ministry identified himself without reserve with the poor, i.e., those unable to repay you for your kindness (e.g., Luke 14.11-15). And consider the implications of the King at his judgment seat before those who identified themselves with the hungry, the thirsty, the sick, the naked, the alien/stranger, and the prisoner (Matt. 25.31-45). These and other examples show the intimate connection between the Messiah and the broken of this world.

The Church, therefore, is the ambassador and agent of *this Messiah*, whose rule is called the Kingdom of God. The Church is therefore called to demonstrate in its worship and practice the life of the age to come in the here and now! (cf. through the Great Commandment, Matt. 22.37-40 and the Great Commission, Matt. 28.18-20).

Looking at the early church, you can see the church's hospitality and generosity from its very birth at Pentecost (Acts 2.42-47). Throughout the book of Acts we see the humble character of the ancient-undivided church: it was persecuted, poor, filled with little folk, largely urban, packed with little gatherings of Gentiles, women, children, and slaves! The Church historically has been the source of dramatic acts of justice for the poor and oppressed. And, we were impressive from our very start: the earliest hostels and funeral care provision was made by churches to the needy. We have cared for the sick, the widow, the orphans, and started numerous hospitals and community ministry enterprises. It can easily be argued that the Church has been one of the world's signature institutions that has stood with courage on behalf of the helpless, the vulnerable, the broken, and the defenseless.

I can testify to this truth, even in my own heritage and family as a Black American. The historical Black Church has been one of the key organizations for the well-being and prosperity of the African-American community. Black denominations and associations started the first historically Black colleges, educational centers, and social justice organizations, creating the cache and reservoir of most Black leaders since the time of slavery. It has been an unrelenting voice crying for justice on behalf of the broken and the poor, and gave birth to some of its most famous and impactful leaders, including the Rev. Dr. Martin Luther King, Jr. Virtually no one, either secular or religious, questions the overall importance of the Black church to life and well-being of the Black community.

I can further argue more personally on this point, citing the Black church's influence on my family, especially my father. My father's name was Theodore Roosevelt Davis, born in 1905, a period of time that was particularly difficult to be Black in America. He was named after a president of the United States, as many young Black boys of his day were, as a sign for Black families of their patriotism and commitment to a nation that largely ignored their humanity and rights as citizens. He grew up in the South, as a young man joined the US Army during World War II, and served in the infantry. But, like virtually all Blacks who served in WWII, my father offered his services to a country that refused to recognize his basic humanity, in a country that segregated his living conditions, shut him out of the political, business, and social realm, and refused him participation even in the GI Bill.

He married my mother, had a passel of children, and became an un-unionized meat packer in a Midwestern ghetto community living in a tough yet proud community.

My father suffered *defacto* and *dejure* denial of his rights on every front, excluded intentionally from full participation in larger society: work, school, society. After living a full but difficult life, my father died the very year our nation guaranteed people like him the right to vote: 1965.

As I ponder the life of my father, I can say that although his treatment was often brutal and unjust, he grew up as a happy man, a family man, and a churchman. He lived with dignity (though he was treated as one not having it), and he provided for us as a follower of Christ, loving my mother and the eight children till the very day he died. As I survey his life, I can testify of all the organizations and connections my family had, there was a single place in America that refused to define him by his color, or deny his rights because of weird social norms and ideas. What was it?

The one place where my father and other adult Black men and women could go and affirm their full rights and commitments as human beings was the church of Jesus Christ! The church, Grant Chapel A.M.E., was the one place in my father's orbit that both recognized and made room for his gifting, calling, person, presence, and potential. It allowed my dad to respond with his gifts as a leader and servant, and provided for growth and friendship for our little poor family, struggling for survival in a northern ghetto community. Contrary to Mr. Barna's assertion, Grant Chapel, A.M.E. church, the little local assembly of poor believers, was our hope and vehicle for transformation. We experienced the life of the Kingdom in the relationships of that poor, Black congregation whose pastor could not attend the seminary, or vote, or participate in the body politic. They still experienced the life of the Kingdom.

The first president of World Impact, the parent ministry of TUMI, summed up the importance of the church in the life of poor people when he stated this:

> Planting churches is the only way to transform alienation into hope, and chaos into peace. It was true in the first century and it is true today. If ever there were people who deserved the nurture, love, protection, and affirmation of the Church, it is the urban poor. The Church is one institution that the poor can run themselves – without government, or monied and influential people calling the shots. The Church empowers the poor.[12]

The Church Is Central in the Consummation of God's Salvation Work

Finally, let me argue that the Church will be central in the consummation of God's salvific work. The church is God's agent of the Gospel, the pillar and ground of the truth of the Gospel, the vehicle through which God's reconciliation through Jesus is testified of throughout the world. The church is called to proclaim the Gospel to the nations (Mark 13.10; Matt. 24.14), and must fulfill this mission before the consummation of the age. Of all the nations, institutions, and entities, on earth, we can be confident of the Church's integrity and place in both time and eternity!

Jesus made it plain that his intent was to leave and prepare a place for his people, and once completed, he would return and gather them to himself (John 14.1-6). By the grace of God, it will be the Church that Jesus returns for on that Great Day of consummation, and she will be caught up together to be with the Lord forever (1 Thess. 4.13-18). According to the will of God, the Church will be judged by our risen Lord and receive the reward for our labor at his judgment seat (cf. Rom. 14.7-12; 1 Cor. 3.10-15; 2 Cor. 5.8-10).

Furthermore, it will be the Church that will enjoy sweet communion together with all the saints, living and dead, to dine with Christ at the Marriage Supper of the Lamb, (Rev. 19.6). And the Word is clear: it will be the Church that will reign with Christ in the new heavens and earth, where the will and reign of God will continue forever, through unending days of bliss and joy (Rom. 8.17; 2 Tim. 2.12; Rev. 5.10; 20.4). No other group, entity, nation, organization, or enterprise can take its place, or substitute for her life and mission.

Without a doubt, the Bible testifies that the life of the Kingdom of God is both present and being offered in the midst of the Church. The *Shekinah* (the glory of God) has reappeared in our midst of his people, God's temple (Eph. 2.19-22). We are, today, the people (*ecclesia*) of the living God, the people of Christ from every kindred, people, nation, tribe, status, and culture (1 Pet. 2.8-9). God's Sabbath rest has been found and is being enjoyed and celebrated here, with its freedom, wholeness, and the justice of God (Heb. 4.3-10). The year of Jubilee has come to us in the person of Jesus Christ; now we can experience God's forgiveness, renewal, and restitution in our relationships with others (Col. 1.13; Matt. 6.33; Eph. 1.3; 2 Pet. 1.3-4). Yes, the pledge of God's Holy Spirit (*arrabon*) indwells us: God lives here and walks among us here (2 Cor. 1.20). And, we taste the powers of the Age to Come in our little assemblies: Satan is bound in our midst, the Curse has been broken here, deliverance is experienced in Jesus's name (Gal. 3.10-14).

Scripture declares all these things to be true, today, right here and right now. What's the deal, then? Why are folks so utterly bored with church services, church life, church ministry? Why do so many Bible-believing churches appear so dead, so lifeless, so segregated, frankly, *so mean and judgmental?*

This experience of the shalom of God's eternal Kingdom takes place in the midst of vicious spiritual warfare (Eph. 6.10-18), where our external, internal and infernal enemies (i.e., the world, the flesh, and the devil respectively) resist the reign of God in every respect (1 Pet. 5.8). We herald the Good News of God's reign (*evangelion*) in the Gospel while we fight the good fight of faith, resisting the devil and defying the world powers seeking to render us neutral and helpless. We are invited to participate in the life of the "Already/Not Yet" Kingdom, and we must struggle until the prize is ours (Phil. 3.11-14).

We are meant to be the *Church militant* today. Soon, we will become the *Church triumphant*. But we won't attain it without a fight. The church is central to God's plan, and therefore important to my own life and identity. I cannot become what I am meant to be without her. She has a huge part to play, both in God's plan and me fulfilling my purpose in Christ. I cannot become God's man without her.

Get Your Pretense On:
The Church Is Your Mother – and Your Home

Do you think it is possible to understand who you are and what you are called to do if you ignore the biblical teaching on the Church, and its place and ministry in the world? I don't think so. Every follower of Christ must begin to wrestle with the meaning of his or her life against the backdrop of what God is doing in the world to gather a people to himself. Can I ignore my place in her, the Church, and still understand my place and part in God's plan, the Kingdom?

No, I cannot. God's call to me for personal salvation and ministry involves *demonstration* of the life of the Kingdom in my allegiance to his people. I can't embrace his salvation and reject his folk. I must receive my call to live as a faithful follower of Jesus *in and among his people in a local assembly*, fleshing out in my character, personal life, family responsibilities, and Christian relationships my allegiance to Christ.

If God is my *Father*, then my fellow believers are *my brothers and sisters*, deserving of my love, sacrifice, and protection (1 John 3.16-18; 4.7-8). Let me not claim to be *deep in God* and *shallow or non-existent* in our church life. To do so is hypocrisy itself. We show that we are his disciples when we have love for his disciples (John 13.34-35).

Apply this *immediately*. If you are not a member of an assembly, ask God to lead you, and when he speaks, join yourself to the pastor and members of the church. Befriend those in the community, and ask God for opportunities to build up the body in the midst of the assembly. Our testimony can only be a truly compelling testimony when lived out in the presence of believers, in the midst of Christian community.

You know, there really is plenty good room in the Father's Kingdom. Just know, that when you choose your seat, you won't be there alone. All of us who love the Lord will be there, too.

CHAPTER 4

Put Off, Renew, Put On:
Getting Your Pretense On in Christian Identity

I grew up in a family of champion storytellers. To this day, when my family gathers, we tell stories, some true, some fictional, all "whoppers," slightly altered for theatrical impact and effect.

One of my favorite stories is the often-told story of the Eagle and the Chickens. There are numerous versions of the tale, all told with great verve and life. Here is my version, a fitting little story to introduce a subject of great importance when it comes to getting your pretense on about your place in the Kingdom of God.

A fable is told about an eagle who thought he was a chicken. When the eagle was very small, he fell from the safety of his nest. A chicken farmer found the eagle, brought him to the farm, and raised him in a chicken coop among his many chickens. The eagle grew up doing what chickens do, living like a chicken, and believing he was a chicken.

The healthy eaglet (baby eagle) was completely welcomed as an equal within the overall chicken society. He was adopted into a chicken family, acknowledged by his chicken step-brothers and sisters, and thought, believed and acted as one of their own. He was well adjusted, growing up to be a fine representative of what a chicken should be and do.

He learned all the chicken habits, assumption, and culture, and enjoyed doing the things that chickens enjoy doing: he became a good clucker, he could cackle with the best of them, and though his beak was big (as well as his feet) he liked scratching in the dirt for grits and worms, juking his head around to scoop up seeds, flapping his wings furiously, rising a few feet, and then crash landing down to the ground with dust and feathers flying. He was imprinted with all things chicken, loving all chicken games, lounging at chicken hangouts, being afraid of chicken enemies, and setting chicken goals. He believed in his heart of hearts that he was a chicken, as did all his fellow chickens, who affirmed his chickenhood and total chickenicity.

Later in life, the eagle-who-believed-he-was-a-chicken looked up overhead and was surprised at that huge bird soaring speedily and with no effort on the wind currents with barely a beat of its wide wings. Looking at his fellow chickens, the older eagle asked, "What is that thing up there?!" "That's what they call an eagle", replied a nearby chicken. "That's what we call the 'King of the Birds.' It's not like us; it was born to fly and soar and hunt. We are birds of the ground, built to peck, and cluck, and cackle. It was made for the air, not like us, birds of the coop."

The old eagle-that-figured-it-was-a-chicken heard the explanation, accepted it, as he had all his life, and yet still – he felt a little funny about it. It seemed like he should be up there, too. All his friend and family chickens went back to clucking, pecking, and cackling, turning their eyes once more to the ground, digging in the dirt around the coop. The eagle-turned-chicken kept looking up, wondering why he felt so pulled to the big bird of the air.

The End?

This homely little tale gets at the core of TUMI's core ministry intent – we seek to empower eagles-acting-like-chickens to awaken to their true selves, to shift their identities by claiming the truth of Jesus Christ, and placing themselves in a position to learn to fly! Paul's exhortation to the Ephesians in Ephesians 4.20-24, outlines a biblical strategy for learning to get your pretense on. In the previous chapters we looked at the Story of God through the lens of the Kingdom and the Church. Now, informed by what the Lord God is doing in the world and in creation, we are in a better position to understand who we are and what we are called to do. You can discover your place in the midst of God's work, and by getting your pretense on, you can allow yourself to begin to think, act, and speak in ways that correspond to who you really are, and not the way you've been conditioned and socialized. You can be who you truly are (an eagle) and not what you've been conditioned to become (a chicken).

In this chapter we will look at Ephesians 4.20-24 seeking to make sense of three, interconnected truths related to our development of a Kingdom, Christ-centered identity. First, we must *teach the eagle that he's not and never was a chicken* (Paul's "put off the old man with its evil desires"). Second, we must *disciple the eagle in God's design for eaglehood* (Paul's "be renewed in the spirit of your mind"). Finally, we must *challenge the eagle to start acting like he truly is an eagle, everyday in every way* (Paul's "put on the new man, created by God's likeness). These three steps of putting off, renewing our mind, and putting on constitutes what it means to live into your true identity in Christ, to "get your pretense on."

And, as we learn to live in this three-step obedience to Paul's teaching we will notice a marked change in both how we perceive ourselves, and how we act in response to circumstances, others, and opportunities that come our way.

Step One
Teach the Eagle That He's Not and Never Was a Chicken:
Put Off Your Old Self with Its Evil Desires

> But that is not the way you learned Christ! – [21] assuming that you have heard about him and were taught in him, as the truth is in Jesus, [22] to put off your old self, which belongs to your former manner of life and is corrupt through deceitful desires.
>
> ~ Ephesians 4.20-22

Paul has just described in Ephesians 1-3 the incredible status and position of the believer in Christ. We are blessed with all spiritual blessings, united to Christ in his resurrection, and saved from our past as children of disobedience and children of wrath. Christ has broken down the wall of division between Jew and Gentile, and the Holy Spirit has placed all believers into fundamental relationship as God's temple, with Jesus Christ being the cornerstone and the prophets and the apostles as the foundation. We have been brought, as Gentiles, into the mystery of God in Christ, who now unites us with the entire family of God, able to do abundantly beyond everything that we ask or think through the power that works within us. This idea is glorious, majestic, and incredible. Perhaps no other place in Scripture is the believer's position in grace so thoroughly and eloquently described as by Paul to the believers in these three truth-packed chapters of affirmation and truth.

According to Paul in Ephesians 4.20-22, we who believe have heard the truth of this majestic position of grace, and we have been taught the truth in Jesus which directly contradicts the old, tired lies and lusts of our Gentile pre-Christian lives. Paul now exhorts us to put off these false, pre-Christian identities, lifestyles, and perspectives of our "old selves," the people we use to be before we confessed faith in Jesus Christ, when we were unsaved.

Paul calls for all believers to consciously reject the old ways of self-talk, self-concept, and self-definition that we had before we met the Savior. Whatever it was, whatever we were called, whatever labels others used about us – all of this is now to be disregarded in favor of the truth in Jesus Christ. According to Paul, our position has changed, and therefore we ought now never accept the same old tired judgments we and others had about who we were and what our lives were about. Since we have believed, we now are rooted in a new direction and philosophy: we have "learned Christ" (vv. 20-21). Our salvation in Christ has provided us with an entirely new foundation of our self-definition: we possess a brand new identity. We are not to treat ourselves as the same person we were before we came to Christ.

As a matter of fact, we are to "put off" (discard, snatch off, lay aside) our old identities which belong to our former manner of life (v. 22a). Like old, shabby clothes, moth-eaten and moldy, we are to "Let all bitterness and wrath and anger and clamor and slander *be put away from you*, along with all malice" (Eph. 4.31). Paul affirms this same attitude of rejecting past perspectives and behaviors in other places where he discipled growing Christians (cf. Col. 3.8 – But now you must *put them all away*: anger, wrath, malice, slander, and obscene talk from your mouth). Christians are not obligated to be consistent with what they used to be; we are new creations (2 Cor. 5.17), the workmanship of God (Eph. 2.10), carrying no obligation to act consistent with our former way of living, speaking, and thinking. We are charged to *lay aside* those things which bound our lives, clogged our minds, and poisoned our hearts. In Christ, through his blood and his grace, we have been set free. We do not need to be what we were any longer. With the indwelling Spirit of God, if we walk in the Spirit we will not fulfill the lusts of the flesh.

Two distinct ways of living and responding are now available to a believer, and s/he must determine which way he or she will go. We can now choose not to agree with the lies about us, about who we are, and what we must necessarily become. Let no one fool you here: the Scriptures exhort us to lay aside the sins that limit, constrain, and spoil us – you don't have to give in to them. You can resist them, and you can win:

> Therefore, since we are surrounded by so great a cloud of witnesses, let us also lay aside every weight, and sin which clings so closely, and let us run with endurance the race that is set before us, [2] looking to Jesus, the founder and perfecter of our faith, who for the joy that was set before him endured the cross, despising the shame, and is seated at the right hand of the throne of God. [3] Consider him who endured from sinners such hostility against himself, so that you may not grow weary or fainthearted.
>
> ~ Hebrews 12.1-3

The writer of Hebrews compares our Christian lives to a race in an arena, with the saints of the ages (those who have finished their race already) cheering us on to the finish. We can lay aside the weights, sins, and lies that hold us back, and learn a new way of running and living. Paul says that our old self, our pre-Christian ways of understanding ourselves and our lives, has been corrupted through wrong desires, all of which are saturated in deceit (lies and falsehoods), v. 22b. The lives we lived before we knew Christ were not informed by the Story of God, or the reversal of God's Kingdom, or the hope of the Church. We lived for empty stuff, wasted our lives and times on things that provided only a temporary measure of relief from the boredom, pain, and rejection of our lives.

However, now that we have come to Christ, we need not embrace the same old lies, lifestyles, and perspectives that led to so much misery and heartache. We have repented and come to the Savior. Now, as believers, God has called us to live out a new identity in Christ that is completely different from our former manner of life (our pre-Christian past), with its worldly and empty assumptions, understandings, beliefs, and convictions.

What does this mean, practically? Well, it means that we need no longer be afraid or ashamed of admitting our errors and mistakes in our past. Now, in Christ we have been forgiven of our sins, cleansed from regret and pain, and can confess that God has forgiven us fully of all the things we have said or done to hurt ourselves or others (1 John 1.6-2.2).

In connection to our lives right now, today, we can affirm that we belong to Christ, as members of his Church, and agents and ambassadors of his Kingdom, called to live out the life Christ won for us in love and grace. We have been called to freedom, set free from guilt, condemnation, blame shifting, and self-hatred, and called to be free to love God and others, from the heart.

Freedom From
Galatians 5.1 – For freedom Christ has set us free; stand firm therefore, and do not submit again to a yoke of slavery.

Freedom to
1 Peter 2.16 – Live as people who are free, not using your freedom as a cover-up for evil, but living as servants of God.

Learning to live in this freedom is one of the primary privileges and responsibilities of every follower of Christ. Jesus came to destroy the devil's work (1 John 3.8), to set us free from our futile effort to please God on our own, to work out our own meaning of life, and to accomplish things that might lead to our own love of ourselves. We can give up the futile attempts to "be somebody" on our own, knowing that God almighty has accepted us in Christ. We need not loathe ourselves, or regret what we've done, or be perpetually dissatisfied in how we look, what we are, and how our "life turned out." God has granted us freedom, a freedom that no one can take away from us, and a freedom that will lead to a new level of love, accomplishment, and proper self-respect.

What is the condition of this freedom and love? Simply to continue in the word of Jesus, to put off the old lies which are filled with deceit, and learn a new way of living based on the truth of God's word. "So Jesus said to the Jews who had believed him, "If you abide in my word, you are truly my disciples, and you will know the truth, and the truth will set you free" (John 8.31-32).

Jacques Ellul sums up this reality of Christian freedom, describing its place in this rejection of the bondage of the old life before we met Christ:

> Freedom is not one element in the Christian life. It is not one of its forms. It does not express itself accidentally, or according to circumstances, or through encounters. In some circumstances temperance is the work of faith, in others faithfulness, in others strict justice, in others extreme clemency. Freedom, however, is not like this. It is not a part or a fragmentary expression of the Christian life. It is the Christian life.
>
> Freedom lies outside the list of virtues. It is not one of the fruits of the Spirit. It is the pedestal on which all the rest can be set. It is the climate in which all things develop and grow. It is the

signification of all acts. It is their orientation. It is the condition of the rest of the Christian life. Freedom is not, then, one of the elements in Christian ethics or morals. Without it there would be no ethics. The Christian life is set within it. . . .

Perhaps this is something which is taken for granted. But the question of the visible and concrete manifestation of freedom is never taken as a starting-point. . . . It is a theme which has vanished from the Christian horizon. The believer is not concerned about knowing whether he is free nor is he worried in the least about ways of manifesting his freedom. In my view this is the very thing that explains the insipidity of the Christian life, its lack of meaning, its failure to make much impact on society. Works of love and service may be multiplied, justice may demonstrated, and faith may be expressed, but none of this is worth anything without freedom.[13]

Putting off does relate to our past, and our present, and also to the way we view and relate to our future. Now redeemed in Christ, free from the tyranny of our past, and released from the obligation to do and be what we used to do and be, we are free to "get our pretense on": we can now act out an entirely new identity, with a new direction, personality, vision, and purpose. We have been called to *glorify God*, and *play our role* in his story, making our contribution in our own unique way and style to God's great redemptive activity.

The following chart is my adaptation of what I take to be uniquely helpful ways to detect and put off the false perspectives and self-talk of both our pre-Christian and current thought patterns. The key to putting off is to recognize the lying pattern that gives birth to the falsehoods that you may routinely and automatically tell yourself. H. Norman Wright developed this remarkable summary of the falsehood tactics the enemy uses to confuse and discourage us. It details the prominent ways in which we may distort and poorly map the territory of our inner lives as well as the events and circumstances that we encounter.

Deadly Habits of the Soul: Categorizing Our Distortions about Safety, Security, and Significance	
Filtering	Tunnel vision: looking at a situation through only one element
Polarized Thinking	Looking at everything in extremes and absolute terms
Over Generalization	Drawing big conclusions based on one incident or piece of evidence
Mind Reading	Making huge snap judgments about situations, people, or events
Catastrophizing	"Making mountains out of molehills" Amplifying "what ifs" into fretting
Personalization	Making everything, regardless of the subject or issue, about yourself
Emotional Reasoning	"If you feel something deeply enough, then it simply must be true."
Blame-Shifting	In the midst of any situation, others must be responsible for the problem.
Shoulds	Functioning by a set of inflexible rules or conditions which must be kept
Always Rightness	Most efforts in any exchange is your effort to prove that you are right.

Adapted from H. Norman Wright, *Self-talk, Imagery, and Prayer in Counseling,* Waco Texas, 1986, pp. 66-68.

Putting Off and Its Connection to Life and Ministry

This putting off is an essential skill in learning to get our pretense on, that is, in affirming the truth about ourselves and our lives as given to us through Christ Jesus. In my view, effective discipleship and leadership development is essentially an issue of *biblical truth and identity formation*. Of course, identity formation flows from *the truth learned in Christ* (i.e., no truth in Christ, no lived-out new identity). Jesus made this plain in addressing some people who only recently believed in him. "So Jesus said to the Jews who had believed him, 'If you abide in my word, you are truly my disciples, [32] and you will know the truth, and the truth will set you free'" (John 8.31-32). This abiding in the Word of God demands that you commit yourself to firmly and courageously confront every falsehood that you become aware of about who you were, who you are, and what you can be.

One of the most difficult things you must learn in putting off is feeling awkward in rejecting ideas that you have embraced and told yourself for years, even throughout your entire life. You must not allow yourself to deal with these perspectives and practices in some strange kind of sympathetic way. Every follower of Christ must learn the importance of *putting off his/her pagan, pre-Christian identity* which was governed by lies and deceit.

This means that we must increasingly become aware of the automatic thoughts that enter into our minds, with their specific messages and absolute terminologies of "must," "always," "never," "should," and "ought." These sentences we say to ourselves must be tested according to the truth, and rephrased, for we tend to "awfulize" the things we face. These thoughts (the old identities and perspectives) must be recognized, rejected, and replaced with the truth. "But test everything; hold fast what is good" (1 Thess. 5.21). J. A. Motyer is correct when he says that "to know" is not a mere exercise of the head. Nothing is "known" until it has also passed over into obedience.[14] We must first learn to put off the old self with its deceit and falsehoods. That is the first step to forming a biblical, Christ-centered identity.

Step Two
Disciple the Eagle in God's Design for Eaglehood: Be Renewed in the Spirit of Your Mind

> . . . and to be renewed in the spirit of your minds . . .
>
> ~ Ephesians 4.23

Forging identity demands, first of all, the putting off of the old self (identity), which includes monitoring our inner conversation and assumptions evaluated by the truth we have learned in Christ. Paul declares that the next important step is to "be renewed in the spirit of our minds," i.e., affirming courageously and enthusiastically God's declaration of who we are and what we possess as a result of our faith in Christ as our Lord and Savior. Actually, the putting off of the old self *demands this constant, unbroken reprogramming of our minds through the Word of God (the renewal in the spirit of our minds, v. 23).*

What is the nature of this renewal "in the spirit of our minds?" To begin with, this renewal involves a *dual emphasis and activity.* On the one hand, we must *monitor our inner assumptions and judgments*, the ongoing stream of thoughts that we tell ourselves throughout the day. And with this, we must also begin to *test and weigh these assumptions* over against what we know and believe as the truth in Christ in the Scriptures. This two-fold activity (becoming aware of our self-talk, and constantly weighing it according to what God's Word declares) represents the core of what it means to be renewed in the spirit of our minds.

This continuous effort of monitoring and interpreting is key to forging a new identity in Christ. At the core of this effort is our commitment to the truth, which must be continuously affirmed, defended, and emphasized. Because we have been conditioned to speak, think, act, and conduct ourselves consistent with *our previous manner of life*, every believer must relearn how to think, and form new habits of the soul to literally reprogram our minds, our language, and our daily habits. *Eagles-conditioned-to-think-and-act-like-chickens must learn a new way of eagle thinking, i.e., the art of eagle attitude and self-talk.*

This renewal demands first of all that you recognize the power of *your former "habits of mind and soul."* You cannot reprogram your mind if you do not accept your own personal need to both monitor and test your inner conversation. This renewal is as much a *disposition and condition* as it is a particular act. You must cultivate the habit of *interviewing all the rogue thoughts* (*"suspicious characters"*) that enter into your mind. We must admit that many of our former thoughts sabotaged us, confused us, led us astray, and were inspired by the enemy himself. Look at these texts on the devil's strategy against God's people:

> Be sober-minded; be watchful. Your adversary the devil prowls around like a roaring lion, seeking someone to devour. [9] *Resist him, firm in your faith*, knowing that the same kinds of suffering are being experienced by your brotherhood throughout the world.
>
> ~ 1 Peter 5.8-9

> "You are doing the works your father did." They said to him, "We were not born of sexual immorality. We have one Father – even God." [42] Jesus said to them, "If God were your Father, you would love me, for I came from God and I am here. I came not of my own accord, but he sent me. [43] Why do you not understand what I say? It is because you cannot bear to hear my word. [44] You are of your father the devil, and your will is to do your father's desires. *He was a murderer from the beginning, and does*

not stand in the truth, because there is no truth in him. When he lies, he speaks out of his own character, for he is a liar and the father of lies."

~ John 8.41-44

But he gives more grace. Therefore it says, "God opposes the proud, but gives grace to the humble."

~ James 4.6

And the great dragon was thrown down, *that ancient serpent, who is called the devil and Satan, the deceiver of the whole world –* he was thrown down to the earth, and his angels were thrown down with him. [10] And I heard a loud voice in heaven, saying, "Now the salvation and the power and the kingdom of our God and the authority of his Christ have come, for the accuser of our brothers has been thrown down, who accuses them day and night before our God.

~ Revelation 12.9-10

Finally, be strong in the Lord and in the strength of his might. [11] *Put on the whole armor of God, that you may be able to stand against the schemes of the devil.* [12] For we do not wrestle against flesh and blood, but against the rulers, against the authorities, against the cosmic powers over this present darkness, against the spiritual forces of evil in the heavenly places. [13] Therefore take up the whole armor of God, that you may be able to withstand in the evil day, and having done all, to stand firm. [14] Stand therefore, having fastened on the belt of truth, and having put on the breastplate of righteousness, [15] and, as shoes for your feet, having put on the readiness given by the gospel of peace. [16] *In all circumstances take up the shield of faith, with which you can extinguish all the flaming darts of the evil one;* [17] and take the helmet of salvation, and the sword of the Spirit, which is the word of God, [18] praying at all times in the Spirit, with all prayer and supplication. To that end keep alert with all perseverance, making supplication for all the saints [italics mine].

~ Ephesians 6.10-18

These texts reveal that the thoughts we have told ourselves, often times for years, if they are false, have their root in Satan's attempt to undermine and confuse us. He is a liar from the beginning, and he suggests his lies to us which appear in the form of our self-talk day by day. In order to forge a new identity, we must learn how to detect and evaluate our hidden core assumptions about God, ourselves, others, life, and the world. The enemy's falsehoods tend to swirl around these categories of our self-talk, what I call "the big five." Lies deeply held and long-told within us in these five areas have caused immeasurable pain, suffering, and insecurity in millions of peoples lives. We can overcome them with the truth of God!

Patrick Rothfuss has a character in his novel, *The Name of the Wind,* who says the following, that I believe wholeheartedly: "It's like everyone tells a story about themselves inside their own head. Always. All the time. That story makes you what you are. *We build ourselves out of that story."* Yes, we build ourselves out of the story we tell ourselves day after day after day. If we intend to live out the truth in Christ, we must interview every judgment about ourselves, urging "only new identity assumptions and attitudes need apply." Below is a chart to help you start to challenge long-held beliefs about yourself which are not consistent with the Word of God and its testimony of who you have become in Christ.

What kind of sentences do you most often tell yourself inwardly?	
I'm dumb, and limited in what I can learn.	The Lord has granted me intelligence.
I am unattractive to myself and others.	Who I am is more than how I look.
People really don't like me.	I love people and make a great friend.
I don't have any real talents.	Thank you Lord for the talents you have given to me.
My current condition is miserable.	God is so gracious to me.
I'm lonely.	I am never alone or forsaken.
I'm poor, and will always be that way.	God is meeting my every need today.
I don't think I can take any more.	I can face every challenge with God's help.
I'm not a good person.	God now accepts me in his Son.
My health is always poor; I'm a sickly person.	Thank you for watching over my health.
I should avoid trying new things, lest I be embarrassed in front of others.	I can do anything the Lord demands of me, for he will help me.
Things are never gonna change; it will always be like this.	God is able to do anything in any situation. I will trust in him alone.
If people really knew my past, they would reject me right off the bat.	God has forgiven me of all my sins.
I should settle for less than my best.	I want to be all God wants me to be.

In the Appendix *Thirty-three Blessings in Christ*, I list for you several dozen things that happen in the life, status, and position of every new believer the moment they accept Christ as Lord and Savior. These things are true regardless of how you may feel about them, how your kids are acting, what your job is like, or the kind of health issues you currently face. These truths are independently and objectively accurate, and not one molecule of their truthfulness is dependent on how you feel, how things look, what you've done, or what's going on. God's Word does not need your affirmation to be true; you need simply to affirm the truth and unchanging Word of God in order to be transformed!

Paul testified of this truth to the Romans: "I appeal to you therefore, brothers, by the mercies of God, to present your bodies as a living sacrifice, holy and acceptable to God, which is your spiritual worship. Do not be conformed to this world, but be transformed by the renewal of your mind, that by testing you may discern what is the will of God, what is good and acceptable and perfect" (Rom. 12.1-2). You *will* be transformed by the renewing of your mind. Start today, start right now. Commit yourself to changing your identity by affirming God's truth and rejecting the lies of your past.

Learning to integrate these truths into your self-talk, with gratitude, enthusiasm, and praise, can literally change your entire outlook, personality, and identity. Rather than being affected by things as they occur, you can transcend those things by forming the habit of affirming the truth. My colleague and friend, Don Allsman, has written a companion volume to mine called *Think Again*. His work outlines the practical how-tos in establishing new patterns of thinking, speaking, and living to make God's truth come alive in your life.

Renewal of the Mind and Its Connection to Life and Ministry

If you choose to renew your mind, you can begin by following a few simple steps. First, *engage in self-observation of your internal stream of thoughts and self-talk.* You simply must become more aware of your habits of self-talk, i.e., what you habitually tell yourself about yourself and your life as you live it, day by day. The better you identify what you are saying, and learn to challenge those sentences and ideas against what you know to be true in the Scripture, the more you will be set free from the old identities that have plagued you for so long. You must become aware of them so you can begin to see how those falsehoods and beliefs are undermining your life, determining how you react to others, and making sense of the circumstances you are encountering day by day.

Second, you must start to *establish life disciplines to saturate your mind in the truth.* Start your day with a quiet time (or a loud time, if you are like me!) with the Lord, in reading the Scriptures, praying and praise. Carve out weekly time to study God's word, and to discuss it with a friend or mentor. Set up a simple, doable plan to begin to begin to memorize the Scriptures, and learn how to meditate on the truth of your new identity in Christ.[15]

Finally, *be patient.* Remember, you have conditioned yourself in certain kinds of self-talk and ways of speaking and seeing things for years, and those years of thinking have conditioned you to respond and react to things in a defined, programmed way. God here is saying that we change, we are transformed, as we put off the old ways of thinking and self-talk, and be renewed in the spirit of our minds by living consistent with the Word of God. We begin to get our pretense on; this won't happen overnight, but it will occur! Give yourself time to form new habits of thinking, new ways of talking, and different ways of responding. The more we do this, the more we will reprogram ourselves into what we truly are – we will become our true selves in Christ. *You were reborn for this, and it will occur, if you simply do not give up.*

Listen and learn from the apostle Paul's exhortation to the Galatians:

> Do not be deceived: God is not mocked, for whatever one sows, that will he also reap. [8] For the one who sows to his own flesh will from the flesh reap corruption, but the one who sows to the Spirit will from the Spirit reap eternal life. [9] And let us not grow weary of doing good, for in due season we will reap, if we do not give up. [10] So then, as we have opportunity, let us do good to everyone, and especially to those who are of the household of faith.
>
> ~ Galatians 6.7-10

We will reap what we sow. (See the Appendix on the *Laws of Sowing and Reaping*.) Have no fear; if you relearn how to sow to the Spirit through new habits of telling the truth, literally reprogramming your mind to be consistent with the Word's testimony about who you are, you will reap life. Don't grow tired in learning this, for, if you persevere, you will reprogram your mind and heart, but you must not quit.

Step Three
Challenge the Eagle to Start Acting Like One:
Put On the New Self Created after the Likeness of God

> . . . and to put on the new self, created after the likeness of God in true righteousness and holiness.
>
> ~ Ephesians 4.24

We come now to the final step in forging and reprogramming our identity: putting on the new self, the very one that has been created in the likeness of God in true righteousness and holiness. This step is the crowning end of our work of rejecting our former lives and reaffirming the new life that Christ won for us on the Cross. To forge a new identity demands, first, that we put off the old self, and then be renewed in the spirit of our minds. Lastly, and perhaps most importantly, we must *put on (i.e., to clothe oneself with) the new self, our new identity in Christ.* This may also be the most difficult for it will demand that we learn the art of pretense, of acting in a manner consistent with what the Word of God declares, in spite of how we may be feeling or how things appear.

At the very core of the Christian life is the reality of faith, "the assurance of things hoped for, the conviction of things not seen" (Heb. 11.1). This establishes that our faith consists of two interrelated things. We have a sense of assurance, a deep sense of being certain about the things we are hoping for, and a conviction about the reality of things even though we cannot see them with our physical eyes. Because of God's truth, we become assured of what we are hoping for, and though we cling to realities that may not be visible at the time, we still affirm them, appropriate them, cling to and celebrate them. Simply, we have confidence in what we take to be true because God said it is true, and so we *act in a corresponding way*, even if, at first glance, it does not appear to be true. We affirm with Paul that God is true, no matter how things look or what we feel: "By no means! Let God be true though every one were a liar, as it is written, 'That you may be justified in your words, and prevail when you are judged'" (Rom. 3.4).

This putting on the new self is not an act of make-believe or auto-suggestion. We literally put on the new self that God says we are, that God says he has given to us, that God says we were meant to be all along. This involves *speaking and acting in ways consistent with what God has said about you*: who you are, what you have, and to what you are called in Christ. (It is essentially about forming new habits of soul!)

This is extremely difficult to do in our society, largely because of the way we define what it means to be real and authentic. We have been taught in our society that, whatever you happen to be feeling or experiencing, you must admit it, live into it, display it. To be authentic is not that you ignore how you might be feeling or thinking at any given moment. Rather, you must admit it, welcome it, and announce it to others. And, when you do this, you are "keeping it real," "not being a phony," "not feeling one thing and acting like another thing" and so on.

Authenticity is equaled with being true to the feelings, and refusing to go anywhere different than what they are suggesting right now. All attempts at seeing emotion *as the result of thinking is gone*. Real living is admitting and embracing the feelings, no matter how gruesome, false, or weird they may be.

This is why we have such a strange and tragic mix of human interactions in our marriages and families today. If a child *feels* that they no longer want to live a certain way, then the parents should respect the feelings and let it be. If a spouse comes to *feel* that all love and cherishing of the other spouse has escaped, then s/he should embrace the feeling, and seek relief in either divorce or an affair. If you *feel* trapped in a job situation or responsibility that no longer provides joy and fulfillment, even though others might be dependent on you, you are no longer obligated to continue. The primary motivation must always be to be *true to one's own heart and feelings*, the sign of true authenticity. Is it any wonder that so many have been so confused for so long?

Over against this orientation toward *authenticity demonstrated by consistent actions with our feelings*, the Scriptures argue for a putting on a new self based on God's actions for us in Christ. As believers, God created for us a new identity "after his likeness," an identity that displays the righteousness and holiness of the Lord. It is not rooted in how we feel, or in the past, or what others think or say or suggest. We have been rescued in Christ, made new in him, and now we are to flesh this out in how we act and behave.

Paul speaks of this in Romans 6.4: "We were buried therefore with him by baptism into death, in order that, just as Christ was raised from the dead by the glory of the Father, we too *might walk in newness of life.*" He further states that since we have been released from the law, and have died to what held us captive, now we can "*serve in the new way of the Spirit* and not in the old way of the written code" (Rom. 7.6). We have been made new in Christ, we are a *new creation, the old has passed away, and now the new has come* (2 Cor. 5.17). We have died with Christ, risen with him and now we have put on the new self, that is being *renewed in knowledge* after the image of its creator (Col. 3.10). All of this has nothing to do with how we feel, or modern notions of what it means to be authentic, or being consistent with our own idea of what it means to "be true to myself."

We actualize the truth when we speak, act, and conduct ourselves in ways consistent with the truth. We live into our new identity in Christ when we commit to forming new habits of thinking, speaking, and acting that align with what Scripture says about us. We put on a new self, affirming that who we really are now is determined by what God has declared, and what God has promised. We can do and accomplish what God says we can, which frankly is not limited by what we can conceive, or what others say our potential is. God is able to do far more abundantly than all that we ask or think, according to the power at work within us (Eph. 3.20-21).

This is why putting on the new self takes both courage and work. We need to know that we are not acting hypocritically when we act and conduct ourselves in ways that correspond to the truth, even if it doesn't align with our feelings. We walk by these truths, not by what we see or sense (2 Cor. 5.7). We are walking by faith, or, to use C. S. Lewis' phrase, by "good pretense."

To act on the truth of God's word certainly may seem to be hypocritical, that we are pretending to be something that we are not. Shouldn't we always *lean into* what we are feeling, express it fully, and never seek to speak or act differently than what our feelings and hearts are saying to us? Let me remind you again of C. S. Lewis' reflection on this point:

> Why? What is the good of pretending to be what you are not? Well, even on the human level, you know, there are two kinds of pretending. There is a bad kind, where the pretense is there instead of the real thing; as when a man pretends he is going to help you instead of really helping you. *But there is also a good kind, where the pretense leads up to the real thing* [italics mine].[16]

We must act like God is true, more true than how we feel or how things appear. This is the testimony of every person in Hebrews' amazing faith chapter, Hebrews chapter 11. All of the heroes and heroines of the faith essentially *chose to act* on God's Word, even though it might have appeared that his promise had become null and void. They pretended with the good kind, "where the pretense leads up to the real thing." This is the key to spiritual formation and discipleship. We must relearn how to think and to speak and to live consistent with the Word. We must put on the new self, walk by faith, and get our pretense on, acting as if God's word is true – about me and my situation.

Being indwelt with the Holy Spirit, we are never alone (Rom. 8.14-17; Gal. 5.16-24; John 7.37-39). God has created (rebirthed us) with a new identity, made in his own image and likeness. Now, through the power of his indwelling Spirit, he empowers us to be new and different if we simply choose to accept his word and act with good pretense into it. The more we actually act consistent with the Word, the more we become like our good pretense. *This is not being phony; this is the pretense that leads up to the real thing.*

Putting on the New Self and Its Connection to Life and Ministry
Forging identity is an issue of clothing your soul: putting off the old clothing of the former manner of living, renewing the mind, and replacing that old style with the new clothing (cf. Col. 3.8-14). All renewal in this identity formation is in the present tense. In other words, we must every day (all day and evening) be engaged in this putting off-renewing the mind-putting on cycle of faith. Listen to what one commentary said about this putting off and on:

> Between the putting off of verse Ephesians 4.22 and the putting on of verse Ephesians 4.24 stands the other content of the teaching the readers had received, mental renewal (v. Ephesians 4.23). This is necessary because prior to conversion most of them had experienced the mental futility and darkness that characterized the unbelieving Gentiles (vv. Ephesians 4.17-18). *This renewal is apparently continual,* since in contrast to the verbs of putting on and off, which are in the aorist tense, which represents simple action, this is in the present tense [italics mine].[17]

We must engage every day in this forging identity cycle: putting off, being renewed, putting on. This discipline, this habit-formation discipline is God's plan for our transformation. God created the new nature, and has provided the resources for us to forge our new identities in Christ.

Conclusion

Let me ask the question again that this chapter began with: how do you help a eagle-who-thinks-s/he-is-a-chicken live into their true identity? The answer is more clearly seen now: *Tell them the truth. Help them to put off their old self, renew their mind, and put on their new self, day by day by day.* We would need to teach the eagle that he's not and never was a chicken (put off the old man with its evil desires), disciple the eagle in God's design for eagle-hood (be renewed in the spirit of your mind), and challenge the eagle to start acting like one (put on the new man, created by God's likeness).

In our next chapter we will explore the idea of representing Christ, an idea all agents of the Kingdom must understand and embrace.

CHAPTER 5

Representin':
Adopting the Mindset and Lifestyle of a Kingdom Citizen and Christ's Ambassador

Who Is the Best Spy in Modern Film History?

One of my favorite personal past times is to view and follow secret agent movies. I have a goodly collection of them, and view them with great pleasure as often as I have time (which is never enough, for an avid spy fan like myself)!

Perhaps the two most popular spy film series of modern times are *James Bond* and *Mission Impossible*. I have always enjoyed the Bond films (with Daniel Craig, in my humble opinion, being the most believable and best Bond of all the six actors who have depicted Bond in film.) James Bond in the 007 series films is the debonair (i.e., confident, stylish, charming, and yes, dangerous) British agent who is licensed to act in an extreme manner for her Majesty's government. He is simultaneously graceful and the most brutally tough of all her Majesty's agents, and is given the highest level of intractable and dangerous operations of any agent. His escapades send him literally all over the globe, dealing with the ingeniously wicked foes, all determined to bring the world to its knees or to its destruction.

With consummate skill and precision, Bond always seems to anticipate the problems, overcome the lack of resources and support, and stand true in the face of betrayals, injuries, and shortages. Some way or other, he always seems to complete the mission and finish the operation, as well as to "get the girl," and restore his status as the first among all British elite agents. He knows how to represent England, and get the job done.

The other spy in film that has intrigued me for some time is Ethan Hunt, the head of the Impossible Mission Force. Tom Cruise plays the hard-hitting Ethan Hunt, and has appeared in all five films, and is set to resume the next one later in 2018.

The created fictional background of the Ethan Hunt character is vintage Hollywood imagination! Ethan Hunt was raised on a dairy farm in Middlefield, New York, graduated Airborne Training, and was recruited by the CIA into an ultra-secret agency called the Impossible Mission Force. The IMF is the most unique, unconventional "black ops" group ever created, a group so elite that they are allowed to operate with virtually no mandated or neatly outlined procedures or protocols to fulfill their top secret missions. They can do whatever they as a team deem necessary in order to "get the job done," with the proviso that if Ethan Hunt or his team is caught or killed, the Secretary overseeing the IMF will disavow any knowledge of them or their operations. If they are captured or killed, they will be "hung out to dry," without recourse to country or authority.

To put it simply – the IMF team is the best trained and resourced squad on the planet to do the most dangerous black ops jobs anywhere, and are given unlimited resources to get the jobs done, together. Ethan Hunt is the point man of the team.

Now, what do James Bond and Ethan Hunt have to do with getting our pretense on or playing our role in the Kingdom Story of Almighty God?

Actually, they both represent a principle which lies at the core of our understanding of what it means to live as an ambassador of Jesus Christ. I have studied this principle for a number of years, and I have given it the name of *"Leadership as Representation."* The principle of representation, in my judgment, is the clearest way to comprehend the meaning of our Lord's ministry as Messiah and Lord, the Suffering Servant of Yahweh who came to fulfill his Father's mandate to redeem humankind and restore the universe under the reign of God. The central theological meaning of the Messiah is to be the anointed one, the one chosen and elect by God, precious and unique, to accomplish God's will in revelation and redemption. Look at the concept of *God's election* in this sampling of prophesies related to the Messiah:

> For to us a child is born, to us a son is given; and the government shall be upon his shoulder, and his name shall be called Wonderful Counselor, Mighty God, Everlasting Father, Prince of Peace. [7] Of the increase of his government and of peace there will be no end, on the throne of David and over his kingdom, to establish it and to uphold it with justice and with righteousness from this time forth and forevermore. The zeal of the LORD of hosts will do this.
>
> ~ Isaiah 9.6-7

> But you, O Bethlehem Ephrathah, who are too little to be among the clans of Judah, from you shall come forth for me one who is to be ruler in Israel, whose coming forth is from of old, from ancient days.
>
> ~ Micah 5.2

> The LORD says to my Lord: "Sit at my right hand, until I make your enemies your footstool." [2] The LORD sends forth from Zion your mighty scepter. Rule in the midst of your enemies!
>
> ~ Psalm 110.1-2

Therefore thus says the Lord GOD, "Behold, I am the one who has laid as a foundation in Zion, a stone, a tested stone, a precious cornerstone, of a sure foundation: 'Whoever believes will not be in haste.'"

~ Isaiah 28.16

The Spirit of the Lord GOD is upon me, because the LORD has anointed me to bring good news to the poor; he has sent me to bind up the brokenhearted, to proclaim liberty to the captives, and the opening of the prison to those who are bound; [2] to proclaim the year of the LORD's favor, and the day of vengeance of our God; to comfort all who mourn; [3] to grant to those who mourn in Zion – to give them a beautiful headdress instead of ashes, the oil of gladness instead of mourning, the garment of praise instead of a faint spirit; that they may be called oaks of righteousness, the planting of the LORD, that he may be glorified.

~ Isaiah 61.1-3

These texts reveal that, in the economy of God, the Messiah was the chosen one, the agent of God empowered to complete God's mission of winning the world back to him. We know this Messiah to be Jesus of Nazareth, the Son of God, the one through whom God has ushered in his victory and his kingdom life (John 3.16-18)!

It is this principle of God's election and empowerment, of representation, that helps us understand the ministry of the apostles as Christ's messengers, given the mandate to make disciples among all people groups, assured that the Spirit would lead them until the job is done. And, it is this principle that helps every Christ follower comprehend their role in the world, serving as citizens and ambassadors of the Kingdom of God in the places where God has placed them.

In this chapter I will give you a flyover of the principle, and why I think it is critical to understand as we seek to get our pretense on regarding our identity and place in God's kingdom plan. We will first seek to understand the *definition* of representation, then follow the *dynamics* of representation, learn how to persevere through the *difficulties* of representation, and finally see what is involved in adopting the *demeanor* of representation.

Understanding the Definition of Representation

Representation, as a concept understood broadly, relates to the idea of someone standing in the place of another, to further their purposes and interests. Here is a working (although dry and formal) definition of representation:

> To represent another is to be selected to stand in the place of another, and thereby fulfill the assigned duties, exercise the rights and serve as deputy for, as well as to speak and act with another's authority on behalf of their interests and reputation.[18]

Representation is essentially the process of commissioning, empowering, and assessing an agent to act on the behalf of a sending authority, under specific guidelines for specific results. From the beginning of my studies on representation, I have been able to see a correlation between representation and virtually every category of missional representation mentioned in the Bible. Let's illustrate this principle in several biblical roles and responsibilities.

Apostles, Evangelists, and Ambassadors as Representatives of Another

The term *apostolos* (rendered apostle) could be referred to as "one who is sent out by another," (cf. Acts 1.2, 26; 6.2; 8.1; 14.4, 14; cf. 1 Cor. 12.28-29). Apostles are not volunteers – they are called by selection to represent the sender (Rom. 1.1; Acts 1.25;

1 Cor. 9.2), and are called by that sender to suffer on the sender's behalf (1 Cor. 4.9ff.; 2 Cor. 11). Further, apostles had to authenticate their calling through their deeds and words. The original apostles saw the risen Lord (1 Cor. 9.1; 15.7-9; Acts 1.21-22), and believers are converted and churches planted through their work (1 Cor. 9.1-2). They performed signs, wonders, and miracles in the power of the Spirit, in the name of the One who sent them (2 Cor. 12.12), and they laid the foundation for the church through their ministries, writings, and prayers (Eph. 2.20; 2 Pet. 3.2). Clearly, then, apostles do not vote themselves into office, or volunteer to represent. Rather, God selected these unique messengers to give final, authoritative witness to the Son of God in the world. Their ministry, therefore, is unique and God ordained.

The same phenomena can be observed for those named as *evangelists or heralds* of the Good News (messengers). The Greek terms for evangelists (*evangelistes*) means "someone who brings good news (Acts 21.8; Eph. 4.11; 2 Tim. 4.5). Another term for herald (*keryx*) "denotes the person who is commissioned by his ruler or the state to call out with a clear voice some item of news and so to make it known" (David Bennett, *Metaphors of Ministry*, p. 135) (cf. 1 Tim. 2.7; 2 Tim. 1.11). Both *evangellos* and *keryx* presuppose the delivery of a message on behalf of someone else (neither were allowed to make up their own announcements; *faithful proclamation* lies at the heart of their duties). To be an evangelist is to be entrusted with Good News, and the mandate to deliver that News to those for whom the message was intended. It is pure representation.

One further example may be chosen to show the intimate connection between ministry, mission and representation. The concept of *Ambassadorship* is one of the apostle Paul's favorite depictions of his ministry to represent kingdom interests in the world as representation:

Therefore, we are ambassadors for Christ, God making his appeal through us. We implore you on behalf of Christ, be reconciled to God.

~ 2 Corinthians 5.20

. . . and also for me, that words may be given to me in opening my mouth boldly to proclaim the mystery of the gospel, [20] *for which I am an ambassador in chains*, that I may declare it boldly, as I ought to speak [italics mine].

~ Ephesians 6.19-20

Presbeuo means to serve as an authorized representative, to be an ambassador or do the work of an ambassador) (2 Cor. 5.20). An ambassador for Christ speaks in the stead of, the place of Christ, as though God himself was making his own appeal *through the ambassador*. Paul considered himself an "ambassador in chains" (Eph. 6.20). David Bennett's fascinating study of various biblical metaphors in ministry makes this point clear:

As a prisoner in Rome, to which foreign delegates came from far and wide, Paul thinks of himself as an ambassador from the King of kings. The status of the ambassador is generally related to the status of the rule that he represents. *This high honor is therefore a privilege available to the humblest of willing believers* [italics mine].[19]

These three illustrations (apostle, evangelist, and ambassador) show the primacy of representation as a concept in the way the Bible depicts what it means to represent the Father's interests in the world. David Bennett suggests that these three are replicated in virtually every mention of leadership in the New Testament:

Over half of the metaphors chosen by Jesus describe someone who is under the authority of another. Often the word selected is one member of a familiar role pair, such as child (of a father, *pater*), servant (of a master, *kyrios*), or disciple (of a teacher, *didaskalos*). Other images of those under authority include the shepherd (*poimen*) who tends a flock that belongs to another, the worker (*ergates*) hired by the landowner (*oikodespotes*), the apostle (*apostolos*) commissioned by his superior, and the sheep (*probaton*) obeying the voice of the shepherd. It is interesting to note that even though the disciples are being prepared for spiritual leadership in the Church, Jesus places far more emphasis on their responsibility to God's authority, than on the authority which they themselves will exercise. *There is far more instruction about the role of following than about the role of leading* [italics mine].[20]

Jesus as the Perfect Pattern of a Representative of God

After this *the Lord appointed seventy-two others and sent them on ahead of him*, two by two, into every town and place where he himself was about to go.

~ Luke 10.1

The one who *hears you hears me*, and the one who *rejects you rejects me*, and the one who *rejects me rejects him who sent me*.

~ Luke 10.16

While it is clear that representation as a concept is bound up in most of the images of ministry in the Scriptures, Jesus himself most perfectly fulfills the duties of being the emissary of God. His life and ministry reveals a clear pattern of what I will later describe as the principles (process) of representation. For instance, Jesus received an assignment from the Father to lay his life down for his sheep (John 10.17-18). He was resourced and empowered for his mission by God's unbounded entrustment of the Holy Spirit (John 3.34; Luke 4.18). Jesus engaged in the mission with wholehearted and unreserved obedience (John 5.30;

Phil. 2.5-11). Our Lord was judged by the One who sent him to be faithful and true in all aspects of his work (Matt. 3.16-17).

With no respect to himself, Jesus fulfilled his task with perfect compliance with the Father's will, even to the point of death (Phil. 2.5-8). And, as a result of his obedience, he was exalted and rewarded by God for his faithful commission with never ending glory and honor (Phil. 2.9-11). This pattern, which I see as being reproduced in person after person in Scripture, I believe is the pattern for the apostles, and for all who name the name of Christ (Jesus said to them again, "Peace be with you. *As the Father has sent me, even so I am sending you*" [John 20.21]).

This representation was seen in the public witness of his ministry. In the baptism of Jesus, our Lord is confirmed and commissioned as God's Son and representative (Mark 1.9-11), and in the temptation of Jesus, we see Satan's attempt to undermine and challenge that role (Mark 1.12-13). During the public ministry of Jesus (i.e., his exorcisms, teaching, miracles, healings, and prayer) Jesus communicated and verified in open display his role as the anointed One of God, his Messiah and final representative (Mark 1.14-15). The word of Hebrews 1 is correct:

> Long ago, at many times and in many ways, God spoke to our fathers by the prophets, [2] but in these last days he has spoken to us by his Son, whom he appointed the heir of all things, through whom also he created the world.
>
> ~ Hebrews 1.1-2

Let this discussion suffice to say that the Bible, through its depiction of the various offices of ministry and foremostly in the person and work of Jesus, shows ministry and calling as a kind of representation, to be selected to stand in the place of another, fulfilling assigned duties and exercising the rights and privileges of a deputy. Applied to all of us, each one of us is called to speak and act with Christ's authority on behalf of his interests and reputation.

Amazingly, every one of us who clings to Christ in faith has been called to live as his own ambassadors in the world, literally acting as his agents (and not-so-secret!) of the King and his Kingdom! "You are the light of the world. A city set on a hill cannot be hidden. Nor do people light a lamp and put it under a basket, but on a stand, and it gives light to all in the house. In the same way, let your light shine before others, so that they may see your good works and give glory to your Father who is in heaven" (Matt. 5.14-16).

Every Disciple Is an Ambassador of Jesus Christ: Everyone, Everywhere, All the Time

The challenge of representing Christ as his ambassador is a formative objective in the life of every person called by God to salvation. Regardless of your background or training, irrespective of your history or experience, now that you have come to Jesus, you have been called to represent his interests and will, to represent him in all that you say and do. To live as an ambassador is a full-time responsibility. All that is done, said, and accomplished must now be done with your true citizenship in mind, providing the kind of representation of your Homeland that honors and communicates its allegiances and commitments. Nothing you do is for your own sake alone. And this high standard applies to every person who names the Name of him who has placed them in this high office of representing the will of the Kingdom of God. Paul Tripp summarizes this key point well in one of his reflections on the meaning of the term "ambassador" for believers in Christ.

> One of my all-time favorite verses is 2 Cor. 5:20 – "Therefore, we are ambassadors for Christ, God making his appeal through us.

We implore you on behalf of Christ, be reconciled to God" (ESV). The Apostle Paul isn't writing this letter to a seminary class of aspiring pastors before graduation. No, this letter is directed to all Christians, no matter their occupation – pastors, school teachers, personal trainers, garbage collectors, stock brokers, moms, police officers. *Everyone. Everywhere. All the time.*

This should be a basic political review: the job of an ambassador is to represent someone or something. Everything he or she does and says must intentionally represent a leader who isn't physically present. An ambassador isn't limited by forty hours a week, to certain state events, or to times of international crisis. An ambassador is always on call, always representing the king.

In other words, the work of an ambassador is incarnational. Their actions, character, and words embody the king who isn't present. In the same way, the Apostle Paul teaches that God has called us all to function as His incarnational ambassadors. Everything we say and do has import because of the King we represent. This isn't a part-time calling; it's a lifestyle. We represent God's purposes to the people He places in our lives. The primary question on our mind should be: *"How can I best represent the King in this place, with this particular person?"*[21]

This statement accurately describes the calling and responsibility of those called to serve as ambassadors. They have been given the charge to "stand in the stead" of their absent Government and Ruler, to represent the Kingdom in the context of their words, conduct, and relationships. We are ambassadors for Christ, Paul exhorts, with him making his appeal through us. We are his agents called to represent his will, precisely in the situation where he has placed us.

Following the Dynamics (the Principles) of Representation

If you look carefully at the ways in which God and Christ called both men and women to represent his interests in a particular task or mission, you will see a pattern with clear dynamics of that calling. These dynamics or principles constitute the active stages and actions involved in every assignment of responsibility for every person who serves as God's emissary, envoy, or representative. These principles form the body of the actual act of delegation to a representative, and through them we can understand the process of our own unique calling, and our roles in representing Christ and his Kingdom where we live.[22]

Let me briefly describe each stage or principle so you can have a clearer understanding of how God calls and commissions his people to do their work.

Principle 1: The Commissioning

Here a representative receives a formal selection and call to represent. This is the first stage of representation. It involves a formal selection and specific call to represent a legitimate authority in a particular operation, task, or role.

When God desires to get something done, he usually selects a particular man or woman to get it done (e.g., Noah to build an ark, Moses to lead his people to freedom, Esther to free her people, Mary to give birth to Messiah, Jesus to save humankind). This involves an emissary who is *chosen* to be an envoy or proxy. Once the call is made, the selection is confirmed both by the sender and the one sent; it is neither arbitrary or self-determined. It is usually for a very particular role, a specific commission to accomplish something: *to a particular position, task, or mission*, and the call typically includes both *privilege and responsibility*. This call is given with the promise that what is needed to accomplish the mission, will be provided.

A clear example of this principle is Paul's call on the Damascus Road, cited in Acts 9. The Lord told Ananias to go to Paul and confirm the commission to him, and to say:

> But the Lord said to him, "Go, for he is a chosen instrument of mine to carry my name before the Gentiles and kings and the children of Israel. [16] For I will show him how much he must suffer for the sake of my name."
>
> ~ Acts 9.15-16

When Paul recounted his own call by the Lord years later, he testified that his original call included the discovery of the person who stopped him, "Jesus of Nazareth, whom you are persecuting" (Acts 22.8). Afterwards, Paul asked the Lord what he would have him do, and the Lord said "Rise, and go into Damascus, and there you will be told all that is appointed for you to do. Go, for I will send you far away to the Gentiles."(Acts 22.10-11).

If you are a Christ follower, you should know that God has called you to represent Christ and his Kingdom right where you are, where you live and work. You don't need a Damascus Road experience to be called by God. The Lord has called every believer to himself (Rom. 8.28-30), and that calling is secure and certain (Rom. 11.29). We have been called to eternal life (1 Tim. 6.12), to participate in a "heavenly calling" (Heb. 3.1), and are called to press toward the mark of the prize for the high calling in Christ (Phil. 3.12-14). God has a role for you to play in his plan, and he will reveal that to you as you walk daily with him.

Each of us has been given a distinct part to play in God's work, often revealed in the roles that he has granted us to play. We are children and parents, we are spouses and siblings, we are co-workers and associates, and we are bosses and followers. Each of us is called to particular roles and responsibilities, entrusted with duties shaped by our own unique life calling. It is in these unique roles and relationships that God's call is often revealed.[23]

Principle 2: The Equipping

This involves the representative receiving appropriate training, provision, and resources to fulfill the call. It is safe to say that God never calls a man or woman to do or endure anything without providing them with the necessary opportunity, resources, and strength to accomplish that thing. Truly, a representative is an *emissary*, one who is sent by another. S/he is assigned to go somewhere, do something, or fulfill some task. The mission assumes resource, guidance, aid, and support. The task is always accompanied by the necessary resources to accomplish the work. This may involve a range of things: training, gifts, support, and help, especially mentorship and coaching.

Think of Paul again, and his retreat into Arabia immediately after his conversion (Gal. 1.13-24). After violently persecuting the church God set him apart for a work, a specific mission to reach Gentiles with the Gospel. Paul did not go to Jerusalem to hob-nob with the apostles. Rather, he went into Arabia, returning to Damascus. It was three years later that he went to Jerusalem and saw Peter and James. His point was clear: the one who had worked mightily in them to do their job, was working mightily in him to do his.

Whatever it is that God has for you to do, he will provide you with all the open doors, monies, support, counsel, and direction you'll need to get it done! All that you need to accomplish God's will he will provide as you rely on him ("And my God will supply every need of yours according to his riches in glory in Christ Jesus", Phil. 4.19). God will not ask you to represent him in something that he does not give you the strength to accomplish his will.

Principle 3: The Entrustment

This involves a representative being endowed with the authority and power to act on behalf of the sender. This is clearly the case with authority today. Why can a 135-pound female officer bring to a halt all vehicle traffic on a busy six-lane highway during rush hour, with just the wave of her arms? She is the representative of the municipality, the state, or the federal government. As an agent of the government, she has been given the authority as its representative to command obedience in certain situations and conditions. *Her size and strength* is not the issue; it is *the size and strength of the governing authority* that she represents that makes all the difference in enforcing the will of the authority.

Of course, the representative is not given unlimited scope and freedom in their use of their authority. Usually the mission dictates the boundaries and limits attached to the authority given. Usually such acknowledgment is given in a public and/or official ceremony, where the representative is sworn in and/or is deputized with the authority to represent. And, after this confirmation is done, the representative now officially is given the right to represent and is released to do the task.

Paul saw his display of signs, wonders, and miracles in the Holy Spirit as the confirming power of his true call as an apostle of Christ (Rom. 15.15-21). God backed up his call and his ministry with signs of power and divine confirmation. Specifically, he made this point to the Romans:

> For I will not venture to speak of anything except what Christ has accomplished through me to bring the Gentiles to obedience – by word and deed, [19] by the power of signs and wonders, by the power of the Spirit of God – so that from Jerusalem and all the way around to Illyricum I have fulfilled the ministry of the gospel of Christ.
>
> ~ Romans 15.18-19

When the Lord calls us to a task, he supports our ministry, stands behind us, and provides the resources needed to get it done. He bears witness alongside us as we bear witness to his work. "How shall we escape if we neglect such a great salvation? It was declared at first by the Lord, and it was attested to us by those who heard, *while God also bore witness by signs and wonders and various miracles and by gifts of the Holy Spirit* distributed according to his will (Heb. 2.3-4). God will stand with us in every task he gives us to do.

Principle 4: The Mission

After receiving God's call, and being equipped and entrusted with authority and supply to accomplish God's will, then the representative is charged with the faithful execution of the task. The agent is now free to engage in the operation in order to accomplish the particular results of the job, according to the specifications and deadlines given.

A representative must *subordinate* his/her will in order to fulfill the task. You have been given a task, and God has given you freedom to accomplish it. Now, go do it! Obedience is the mark of a faithful representative, and the key virtues of a representative are loyalty, integrity, and wholehearted engagement. The mission is about *achieving results*, not about *possessing intentions*. God calls his folk to do his will, and in the doing, there is blessing!

Jesus exemplifies this principle as Messiah of God, carrying out his task of fulfilling the Father's plan. He constantly spoke of his commitment to do his will. Throughout his life and ministry, he spoke of his intent to accomplish the will and call of God.

> Consequently, when Christ came into the world, he said, "Sacrifices and offerings you have not desired, but a body have you prepared for me; [6] in burnt offerings and sin offerings you have taken no pleasure. [7] Then I said, 'Behold, I have come to

do your will, O God, as it is written of me in the scroll of the book'" [quotation of Psalm 40.6-8].

~ Hebrews 10.5-7

Jesus said to them, "My food is to do the will of him who sent me and to accomplish his work."

~ John 4.34

"I can do nothing on my own. As I hear, I judge, and my judgment is just, because I seek not my own will but the will of him who sent me."

~ John 5.30

So Jesus said to them, "When you have lifted up the Son of Man, then you will know that I am he, and that I do nothing on my own authority, but speak just as the Father taught me."

~ John 8.28

I glorified you on earth, having accomplished the work that you gave me to do.

~ John 17.4

Jesus was the perfect representative of God, and accomplished the will of God in every respect. Like him, we are called to have the same mind, the same inclination and spirit, to give ourselves to do the tasks that he has called us to do. We are to "Have this mind among yourselves, which is yours in Christ Jesus (Phil. 2.5), who emptied himself, took on the form of a servant, and was obedient to death, dying on the cross for us" (Phil. 2.6-8).

Principle 5: The Reckoning
Every representative is answerable to the one who sent him/her, and their work will be assessed by the one who sent him or her. The representative answers back to the sending authority, whose actions are weighed against the results requested. The work of every agent must be evaluated and reviewed. Usually the

evaluation and review time is formal, comprehensive, and decisive. The agent's *work product* as well as their *personal predisposition during the work* are evaluated, and they are rewarded, based on their performance.

Paul spoke often of his answerability before God of the work that he had been called to do. He used the analogy of the *bema seat*, the place in the ancient municipalities where actions were weighed and judgments given regarding the facts of a case. He taught that each believer will need to stand before the *bema seat* of Christ, to receive directly from the Lord the blessings and or judgment for the work they did, in answer to their particular call. (This judgment is not concerning eternal life, but regarding reward for faithfulness in answer to God's specific call on our lives.)

Whatever you do, work heartily, as for the Lord and not for men, [24] knowing that from the Lord you will receive the inheritance as your reward. You are serving the Lord Christ. [25] For the wrongdoer will be paid back for the wrong he has done, and there is no partiality.

~ Colossians 3.23-25

According to the grace of God given to me, like a skilled master builder I laid a foundation, and someone else is building upon it. Let each one take care how he builds upon it. [11] For no one can lay a foundation other than that which is laid, which is Jesus Christ. [12] Now if anyone builds on the foundation with gold, silver, precious stones, wood, hay, straw – [13] each one's work will become manifest, for the Day will disclose it, because it will be revealed by fire, and the fire will test what sort of work each one has done. [14] If the work that anyone has built on the foundation survives, he will receive a reward. [15] If anyone's work is burned up, he will suffer loss, though he himself will be saved, but only as through fire. [16] Do you not know that you are God's temple and that God's Spirit dwells in you?

~ 1 Corinthians 3.10-16

Why do you pass judgment on your brother? Or you, why do you despise your brother? For we will all stand before the judgment seat [*bema seat*] of God; [11] for it is written, "As I live, says the Lord, every knee shall bow to me, and every tongue shall confess to God." [12] So then each of us will give an account of himself to God.

~ Romans 14.10-12

Each of us is provided a specific calling and mission, with resources and gifts given that we may glorify God in our work. Jesus will assess the quality of our works, not to condemn us, but to reward us for the faithful service we have done for him, in his name and honor.

Moreover, it is required of stewards that they be found trustworthy. [3] *But with me it is a very small thing that I should be judged by you or by any human court. In fact, I do not even judge myself.* [4] I am not aware of anything against myself, but I am not thereby acquitted. It is the Lord who judges me. [5] *Therefore do not pronounce judgment before the time, before the Lord comes, who will bring to light the things now hidden in darkness and will disclose the purposes of the heart. Then each one will receive his commendation from God* [italics mine].

~ 1 Corinthians 4.2-5

Principle 6: The Reward
Every representative is recognized and rewarded on the basis of his/her faithful service and obedience to the sender, and the

accomplishment of their task. This final principle is intimately connected to the review principle above. The results that a representative accomplished are reviewed, and when they have been found to be faithful, they are often publicly acknowledged. The sender acknowledges and recognizes the behavior, conduct, and product of the representative's actions, and the reward and recognition corresponds to the level of faithful obedience to the task.

If a representative is found to have done well, they are usually rewarded with new levels of responsibility and authority, depending on the level of faithful execution of the task. If they did remarkably well, they received great reward, and if they did reasonably well, they received lesser reward.

This cycle of representation (commissioning, equipping, entrustment, mission, review, and reward) is cited throughout the Bible, with Old Testament and New Testament characters alike, and fills the parables of our Lord. Jesus referred to this cycle often in his teaching, i.e., of a master entrusting a task to his servants who are allowed to do work, and then, at its end, receive a reward for the quality of work they performed. This cycle is fully displayed in Jesus's parable of the Talents, in Matthew 25. Here are a few highlights of this important teaching:

> For it will be like a man going on a journey, who called his servants and entrusted to them his property. [15] To one he gave five talents, to another two, to another one, to each according to his ability. Then he went away.
>
> ~ Matthew 25.14-15

> Now after a long time the master of those servants came and settled accounts with them. [20] And he who had received the

five talents came forward, bringing five talents more, saying, 'Master, you delivered to me five talents; here I have made five talents more.' [21] His master said to him, "Well done, good and faithful servant. You have been faithful over a little; I will set you over much. Enter into the joy of your master."

~ Matthew 25.19-21

His master said to him, "Well done, good and faithful servant. You have been faithful over a little; I will set you over much. Enter into the joy of your master." [24] He also who had received the one talent came forward, saying, "Master, I knew you to be a hard man, reaping where you did not sow, and gathering where you scattered no seed, [25] so I was afraid, and I went and hid your talent in the ground. Here you have what is yours." [26] But his master answered him, "You wicked and slothful servant! You knew that I reap where I have not sown and gather where I scattered no seed? [27] Then you ought to have invested my money with the bankers, and at my coming I should have received what was my own with interest. [28] So take the talent from him and give it to him who has the ten talents. [29] For to everyone who has will more be given, and he will have an abundance. But from the one who has not, even what he has will be taken away."[24]

~ Matthew 25.23-29

We need not fear the judgment seat of Christ, for those who confess Jesus as Lord and believe in their hearts that God has raised him from the dead will certainly be saved (Rom. 10.9-10). This review and reward is concerning Christ's recognition and commendation for our faithful discipleship, not to determine if we are saved or not. Still, the idea that each of us has the opportunity to so live and work for him to hear is "Well done, good and faithful servant" should inspire us to get our pretense on, and to keep it on, day by day.[25]

Persevere through the Difficulties of Representation

To represent another is difficult, filled with challenges and stress. When you have been given a job to do, it is important to be aware that the fulfillment of the task will often not be easy. There will be inward irritations, the difficulties of conscience, conviction, and character.

Everyone sometimes struggles with the confidence of *conscience*: *What do you do when you reach a crisis of conscience in representing your sender?* "The aim of our charge is love that issues from *a pure heart and a good conscience and a sincere faith*" (1 Tim. 1.5). Being asked to do something that is difficult or costly can easily grate against your conscience, like when you do not feel good about doing what is demanded of you. Persistent doubt in your ability can create inaction, and not feeling like you can do it can discourage you.

What about the clarity of *conviction*: *What do you do when your own personal belief system conflicts with what your sender wants you to do?* We struggle sometimes knowing what it is precisely that God wants us to do. What do you do when everybody is advising you on a course of action and nothing seems clear? To obey God's call means that you must be fully convinced yourself of what he is calling you to be and do. Scripture study, pastoral counseling, prayer, spiritual director and mentor input, and circumstances are all things that God can and will use to provide you direction on where he wants you to go. (One person esteems one day as better than another, while another esteems all days alike. *Each one should be fully convinced in his own mind* [italics mine], Rom. 14.5).

Finally, we must also face the challenge of our developing *character*: *How does one's character shape and affect the kind of representation that you offer to your sender?* Paul instructed Timothy in 2 Timothy

2.1-7 that he needed to watch his own character, for it could greatly impact his obedience and service to Christ. He told him to share in suffering as a soldier, not getting entangled in civilian pursuits. Like an athlete he should compete according to the rules, and like a farmer, be patient and yet share in the produce of the crops. A willingness to suffer, to follow God's rule, and to be patient – our character greatly shapes our ability to represent Christ and his Kingdom where we live.

These three difficulties – issues of conscience, conviction, and character – can shape the way we serve Christ. We must be aware of our own ability to undermine God's call, and the enemy's desire to sabotage us as we seek to fulfill God's will in the roles and responsibilities God has granted us.

Adopt the Demeanor of an
Ambassador and Agent of the Kingdom

All this reflection on representation brings us to the end: the need for each of us to accept our position as *an agent and ambassador of the Lord*. The great take-away from this teaching should always be the wonder of the honor that we have been given to represent Christ and his Kingdom in the unique circle of relationships and responsibility that he has granted to us.

As Jesus was a representative of the Father who fulfilled with perfect obedience and flawless accuracy precisely what the Father wanted him to do (Phil. 2.5-8), now he has called us to be his representatives where we live and work ("Jesus said to them again, 'Peace be with you. As the Father has sent me, even so I am sending you,'" John 20.21). We have become a thread in the sacred tapestry of those granted the privilege of standing in the place of the risen Lord. You are his agent, right in the place where he has placed you. Hear the words of the apostle Paul on this very point:

Only let each person lead the life that the Lord has assigned to him, and to which God has called him. This is my rule in all the churches. [18] Was anyone at the time of his call already circumcised? Let him not seek to remove the marks of circumcision. Was anyone at the time of his call uncircumcised? Let him not seek circumcision. [19] For neither circumcision counts for anything nor uncircumcision, but keeping the commandments of God. [20] Each one should remain in the condition in which he was called. [21] Were you a bond-servant when called? Do not be concerned about it. (But if you can gain your freedom, avail yourself of the opportunity.) [22] For he who was called in the Lord as a bond-servant is a freedman of the Lord. Likewise he who was free when called is a bond-servant of Christ. [23] You were bought with a price; do not become bond-servants of men. [24] So, brothers, in whatever condition each was called, there let him remain with God.

~ 1 Corinthians 7.17-24

This passage has often been misinterpreted as suggesting that Paul wanted oppressed peoples to stay in the lowly, ignoble roles they possessed when they believed. Such a view argues that we should not seek to better our social positions but mindlessly stay "under the thumb" of our unjust masters in the abusive conditions we live in, all for the sake of the Gospel.

Nothing could be further from the truth! Paul here is rather exhorting believers to recognize their God-called, unique, and special place as those purchased by God and commissioned to represent the Kingdom, *wherever we are*. Paul recognizes the unique calling of every person, despite their social position, and argues that in that particular space, we can represent Christ with honor and advance his kingdom interests, even in the places where we live when we accept Christ as Lord. Every believer is an agent of the Kingdom, every disciple can minister the life of the Good News in the place where God has placed them today.

Correspondingly, we do not need to be in "full time ministry"; every role and life where we are is "full time ministry." Our position, station, or employment status does not matter. We can be carpenters, teachers, plumbers, or accountants. We can be married or single, young or old, poor or wealthy, graduates of the IVY league, or learned our craft on the streets or in the prison yard. We can be a minister and church planter, or a sales person or a roofer. We can be housewives (or house-husbands), supervisors or shop fellows, foremen and forewomen, a grand-mother, or an uncle or aunt, secretaries, or students, or politicians – or *whomever*.

The issue here is this: it is not where you might be, but *how you live and act* where he has placed you. The Lord needs ambassadors in the board room and on the shop floor, in the sales office and in the college classroom, in the halls of power and on the streets of the people.

You must deliberately live with your new identity as God's agent and ambassador. Change your persona (in other words, match your *demeanor* with your *designation*). *Get your pretense on!* Do not be colloquial or causal about your role as Christ's agent and "missionary" where he has placed you. Embrace your identity as *his Gospel representative* with those with whom you represent and relate. Let everything you do (your words, disposition, attitude, and actions) show you to be Christ's servant and agent.

Represent the Kingdom, live by its purposes, priorities, and principles. And, above all be patient with yourself. Give yourself time to try on your new persona and identity as Christ's ambassador to the people and place where he has assigned you. Do not forget C. S. Lewis' wise counsel about the *good kind* of pretending, where *the pretense leads up to the real thing*. You are an ambassador of Christ in your life situation; now, starting acting like it. Before long, you will see the change in yourself, and the impact you are making for the Kingdom, where you live and work.

CHAPTER 6
The *Oikos* Factor:
Being Used of God to Change Your World

One of the most intriguing stories among the many in the book of Acts is the encounter Paul and Silas had with the Philippian jailer and his household. It demonstrates vividly the most powerful, natural, and effective way for us to serve as ambassadors of Christ, and the way that the Good News penetrates the families and households of people in society. Here in extended quote is that episode in Acts 16:

> But when her owners saw that their hope of gain was gone, they seized Paul and Silas and dragged them into the marketplace before the rulers. [20] And when they had brought them to the magistrates, they said, "These men are Jews, and they are disturbing our city. [21] They advocate customs that are not lawful for us as Romans to accept or practice." [22] The crowd joined in attacking them, and the magistrates tore the garments off them and gave orders to beat them with rods. [23] And when they had inflicted many blows upon them, they threw them into prison, ordering the jailer to keep them safely. [24] Having received this order, he put them into the inner prison and fastened their feet in the stocks. [25] About midnight Paul and Silas were praying and singing hymns to God, and the

prisoners were listening to them, [26] and suddenly there was a great earthquake, so that the foundations of the prison were shaken. And immediately all the doors were opened, and everyone's bonds were unfastened. [27] When the jailer woke and saw that the prison doors were open, he drew his sword and was about to kill himself, supposing that the prisoners had escaped. [28] But Paul cried with a loud voice, "Do not harm yourself, for we are all here." [29] And the jailer called for lights and rushed in, and trembling with fear he fell down before Paul and Silas. [30] Then he brought them out and said, "Sirs, what must I do to be saved?" [31] And they said, "Believe in the Lord Jesus, and you will be saved, you and your household." [32] And they spoke the word of the Lord to him and to all who were in his house. [33] And he took them the same hour of the night and washed their wounds; and he was baptized at once, he and all his family. [34] Then he brought them up into his house and set food before them. And he rejoiced along with his entire household that he had believed in God.

~ Acts 16.19-34

"You and Your Household": The Road into the Kingdom

As spoken in the last chapter, we who believe have been called to be Christ's ambassadors, his own "secret agents" in the place where he has put us, serving as his own called-and-gifted representatives of his Kingdom in the circle and sphere of relationships we now indwell. As a son or daughter, a husband or wife, an employee and friend, a neighbor and associate (or whatever other roles you play in your life) God has granted to us the opportunity to share Christ with these dear folk. To pray for, relate to, and bear witness to Christ in these personal circles, in the most natural and personal way, deals with *the principle of oikos*, or circle-of-life evangelism. An *oikos* is a web of common kinship relationships, friendships, and associations that make up a person's larger social circle. Sharing the Gospel in word and deed in the context of our *oikos*

relationships is perhaps the most natural and effective means
to spread the Gospel with the lost, wherever they live.

The story of Paul and Silas and the Philippian jailer highlights
the power of *oikos* evangelism. This story is the last episode of Paul
and Silas' witness in the region of Macedonia, and in the leading
city of that region, Philippi. As a result of their effective ministry
there, with the first convert in Europe (Lydia and her "household,"
oikos, Acts 16.14ff.), Paul and Silas ran into trouble with false
accusations of being religious profiteers, and were thrown into
prison. After being beaten by the jailer with "many blows," they
were thrown into prison with their feet bound in stocks. Around
midnight, these dear brothers were praying and singing hymns
of praise to God, with the other prisoners listening in. Suddenly,
a great earthquake shook the foundations of the prison house.
All the doors opened and everyone's chains were unfastened – the
power of prayer and praise of God's servants in trouble!

When the jailer awoke and saw all this, he thought to draw his
sword (believing that the prisoners had escaped), but Paul cried
out with a loud voice for him not to harm himself for "we are all
here!" The jailer called for lights, fell before Paul and Silas, and after
bringing them out of the prison, asked them what he needed to
do to be saved. Paul and Silas' answer is as potent today as those
centuries ago: "Believe in the Lord Jesus, and you will be saved,
you and your household [*oikos*]."

Simple faith in the risen Lord Jesus is sufficient to deliver us from
wrath, break the power of condemnation and guilt, justify us before
God as righteous, and ensure us of eternal life, commencing from
the moment we declare Jesus as Lord of all, and Lord over our lives.
Paul and Silas spoke the word of God to the jailer, and to all the
members of his *oikos*, that network of family, friends, and associates
connected to the jailer through trusting relationships and ongoing
contact. Not only did the jailer repent and believe on the Lord Jesus,

being baptized by Paul and Silas, but "all his household" as well. They ate together that night, rejoicing as an *oikos* that they had believed in God. In one meeting, the entire family, friendship, and associate network of the jailer entered the Kingdom through faith in Jesus Christ.

This incident highlights the most natural, direct, and most effective way for the Gospel to spread. Each one of us is connected to others, by birth, proximity, or by some relationship that connects us to a network of people who know, recognize, and associate with us. These networks represent the "fabric of our lives," the web of relationships that provide us with identity, friendship, and connection. This story illustrates the power of the Gospel to penetrate society, and reveals how the Good News spreads through the work of the apostles. Through their web of influence, their network of relationships, the Good News touched every strata of society, every corner of the Roman empire. We marvel at the work of God through the apostles, as we should. We also should look carefully at the natural, spontaneous, and very real way the Gospel spreads – along the lines of real family, friendships, and associates.

Go and Make Disciples . . . in the 'Hood'

> And Jesus came and said to them, "All authority in heaven and on earth has been given to me. [19] Go therefore and make disciples of all nations, baptizing them in the name of the Father and of the Son and of the Holy Spirit, [20] teaching them to observe all that I have commanded you. And behold, I am with you always, to the end of the age."
>
> ~ Matthew 28.18-20

One of the most basic traits of our global societies today (and especially so in our modern urban poor neighborhoods) is the reality of distrust and suspicion. The ongoing theme is: "Don't get played by others! *"Everybody's got a game, and if you don't watch out, they'll play it on you!"* Our world is dramatically fractured today. Many nations and regions are openly hostile to the Gospel, refusing to let missionaries and evangelists do the work of Christ in their countries and provinces. It is difficult (and can be dangerous) to cross barriers of race, gender, culture, class, and ethnicity within many neighborhoods, which look on "outsiders" with great suspicion and distrust.

Our urban neighborhoods, too, make it difficult to penetrate new relationship networks. Our family units tend to be broken and disjointed, our economic situation is underserved and underdeveloped, and many of our residents suffer from alienation and loneliness. Many of the urban poor communities are plagued with violence and crime, with problems with relations with the police and law enforcement, and many households are caught up in the system of the courts, prison, and the law. Add to that the overall general sense of despair and distrust, and you have a perfect recipe for communities unlikely to listen to or relate to strangers *for any reason*, let alone for issues of "the church."

As an ambassadors for Christ and his Kingdom, the question for you and me will always be the same. *How do we connect with people in their own setting with credibility and openness, when the general environment where we live and work alongside each other is saturated with distrust, fear, and alienation?* I believe that the Lord has given us a solution, a solid answer that we can follow, which was significant in the times of the apostles and can be so today as well. We can share the Good News of life with others as we naturally relate with people *through the oikos networks we already have with our friends, neighbors, associates, and family!*

The Concept of Evangelism, the Family, and *Oikos*
Oikos relates to the most effective way we can engage our urban communities that communicates the Gospel in a credible, effective,

and non-invasive manner. When we look at the Scriptures, one of the first things we find is the notion of *family*, the place of our parental lineage and historical descent. *Patria* is one of the most common concepts in our New Testament. For instance, Joseph is of the *patria* of David, Luke 2.4, and God's promise to us is that all the families (*patria*) of the earth will be blessed in Abraham (cf. Acts 3.25). Almighty God is our Father, from whom the entire (*patria*) in heaven and earth is named (Eph. 3.14-15). Truly, God has placed all human beings in a *patria*, a network of relationships and kinship that is constituted by our *physical and parental lineage.*

One of the great concepts of the Bible is that through our belief in Christ as Savior and Lord, we are made members of the very family of God (1 John 3.1-3), one which we can only enter through a new birth effected by our faith in Christ (John 1.12-13). Our "natural" state before our sonship and daughterhood in the Father through Christ, is our relationship to God's enemy Satan. Those who do not believe are referred to as children of the devil (John 8.44; 1 John 3.10), as children of wrath (Eph. 2.1-3), children of disobedience (Col. 3.6), and children of Adam (Rom. 5.12-21). All of these associations speak to our need to be born from above, from God's own life through faith in Christ through the Gospel (Rom. 10.9-10).

Note Paul's rendering of this concept to the Galatians:

> But now that faith has come, we are no longer under a guardian, [26] for in Christ Jesus you are all sons of God, through faith. [27] For as many of you as were baptized into Christ have put on Christ. [28] There is neither Jew nor Greek, there is neither slave nor free, there is neither male nor female, for you are all one in Christ Jesus. [29] And if you are Christ's, then you are Abraham's offspring, heirs according to promise.
>
> ~ Galatians 3.25-29

When we do, in fact, repent and believe, we become the very children of the Father, sharing in God's own DNA through the Holy Spirit, entering into the family of God through faith in Christ (John 1.12-13). The living instrumentality of the Word of God is that by which we are born from above (1 Pet. 1.22-25), and repentance and faith is the means by which we were born (Acts 2.38-39). The Holy Spirit regenerates us, linking us forever to Christ and his life (1 Cor. 12.13; Titus 3.4-7), and we become God's very own children, members of his family, and heirs with Christ in God (Rom. 8.14-17). The implication of this is clear for all of us: *the picture of the family is one of the central figures of the Spirit to describe the process of repentance, faith, and new birth in Christ.*

Oikos: The Most Common Term for "Family"
The roots of the New Testament concept of family network (*oikos*) is given clearly in the Old Testament. According to Hans Walter Wolff in *Anthology of the Old Testament,* "A household usually contained four generations, including men, married women, unmarried daughters, slaves of both sexes, persons without citizenship, and 'sojourners,' or resident foreign workers." This shows that family included the place of *generational unity* (four generations), the place of *kinship* (immediate and extended family), the place of *commerce and livelihood*: (including servants, workers, and slaves), as well as the place of *association* (sojourners, associates).

This extended understanding of the social network of the Old Testament continued into the intertestamental period, during the life of Jesus, as well as the time of the apostles. The Gospel in our NT narratives is described as *coming through and to* the various people *in the household where they resided* (e.g., Mark 5.19; Luke 19.9). The apostles shared the news of Christ with their brothers and relatives, their friends and associates, in the context of their relationships and life together (John 1.41-45;

John 4.53). Cornelius is a prime example of the role of *oikos* household in evangelism, the subject of extended treatment by Luke in Acts 10-11.

In one sense, all of the ancient cultures had terms to describe the concept of family, which, more or less, referred to the same social units. *Oikos* (Greek) referred to the same unit as *bayit* (Hebrew) as well as to *familia* (Latin). *Oikos* does not refer to our typical Western notion of the family as mother, father, and children (i.e., our nuclear family idea). Rather, *oikos* took on a broader scope, understanding "family" as all the members of a person's "household as social unit," including blood relatives of the head of the house, as well as other dependents (i.e., slaves, employees, and "clients" [freedmen, friends, and others who looked to the head of the household for patronage, benefaction, advancement, or protection]). Correspondingly, the term *oikia* (plural of *oikos*) is also used in the New Testament to signify the property or substance of a particular household (Mark 10.29; Mark 12.40).

When I refer to the term *oikos* in this book I interpret it to mean that *entire network of relationships that we have in our immediate and extended families, our friendships, those connected to our web of contacts and associations.* I am referring to our *oikos* closer to the sense it is used in the Scriptures, rather than our typical way of understanding family as our immediate, nuclear family.

(*Oikos*) and The Gospel in the New Testament

One of the most exciting ways to understand the power of *oikos* is to see how the Gospel spread through family, friends, and associates through networks that followed *oikos relationships*. The Jerusalem church worshiped, was organized, and discipled in the *oikos* networks revealed in the Pentecost conversions (Acts 2.46; Acts 5.42; Acts 12.12). The Good News of Jesus Christ was often shared in the natural settings of people in their web of relationships and friendships, e.g., Cornelius and his household (Acts 10-11; cf. Acts 10.24).

It also appears that the nucleus of most of Paul's missionary planted churches were made up of one or more households (*oikos* networks) where he naturally shared the Good News of salvation (see the households of Lydia and the jailer at Philippi, Acts 16.15; the households of Stephanas, Crispus, and Gaius at Corinth, Acts 18.8; Rom.16.23; 1 Cor. 1.14-16; 1 Cor. 16.15; and the households of Priscilla and Aquila, as well as Onesiphorus at Ephesus (1 Cor. 16.19; 2 Tim. 1.16; 2 Tim. 4.19). This is also true of the *oikos* of Philemon at Colossae (Philem. 1.1-2), Nympha at Laodicea (Col. 4.15-16), and Aristobolus, Narcissus, and others at Rome (Rom. 16.10-11).

What is truly exciting, when looking at the biblical evidence, is that *oikos* households, once converted to Jesus and his Kingdom, could themselves constitute a church. Paul could refer to the "the church (*ekklesia*) which meets in their house (*oikos*)" (Rom. 16.3-5). The various "household codes" in Ephesians and Colossians – husband and wife, parents and children, master and slave – are those who would be a part of a single New Testament *household*. It appears that *oikos* networks were stable enough to provide a nucleus or base out of which a wide group of believers could meet and live under its hospitality. Through these relationships, now Gentile and Jewish believers could be connected intimately through Christ, breaking down historical barriers (gl. 3.28; Eph. 2.19-22). Leaders of the church were to be good managers of their own *oikos* households, since they were called to care for the "household of God" (1 Tim. 3.2-7; Titus 1.6). Truly, the *oikos* became the place where teaching, worship, fellowship, and witness occurred in the early church (Acts 5.42; Acts 20.20), including baptism (Acts 16.15; 1 Cor. 1.16) the Lord's

Supper (breaking of bread) (Acts 2.46), discipleship "house to house" (Acts 20.20), Christian education for children (Eph. 6.4), and discipling of young wives (1 Cor. 14.35).

This overview of the ancient *oikos* excites me greatly! The Gospel spread through the natural lines and links of real relationships already established, in homes, friendships, businesses, associations, schools – in other words, in the flow of the natural connections in life. Today in our urban neighborhoods, we can be led of the Spirit to develop strategies for spreading the Good News that take seriously the natural social units, i.e., the *oikos*, of each person who we seek to reach. We can win an entire *household* through its members, discipling them to share the hope of the Gospel through their own God-given webs of relationships and connections they already know, love, and relate to!

Defining the *Oikos* Today

My own definition of *oikos* today focuses on the power of sharing and relating in the context of our natural web of relationships:

> That natural web of relationships where individuals are recognized and embraced as a part of a larger social unit, based upon common kinship relationships, common friendships, and associations.

Note the elements in this definition; "*Natural web of relationships*" refers to an *oikos* as the most basic and natural web of identity and connection for people. "*Where individuals are recognized and embraced as a part of a larger social unit*" sees an *oikos* as that social unit where individuals are recognized and embraced as a significant member of a larger network of relationships. This means the family or group to which the individual belongs, where they personally make connection and association. This may include their own place of origin, family background and neighborhood, but also include their larger network of friends and community where they are known of and cared for.

The three critical areas of *oikos* connection are *kinship relationships, friendships, and associates*. Kinship refers to our family connections, including our mother and father, whether their birth parents or those who raised and nurtured the person in their infancy and youth. Also, this would include our brothers and sisters (whether by birth or association), our extended family members as well as our "adopted families": i.e., those relationships which operate as family for the individual.[26]

Next, *oikos* includes those who we count as our friends, our "significant others." In the city where I grew up these immediate friends were called our "running partners," your "dawg," those individuals with which we most readily affiliated and connected to, i.e., those folk we counted as "members" of the same crew or group, who share with us our common commitments and/or special interests.

Finally, our *oikos* includes those with whom we naturally associate, whether in proximity (neighbors), work, or play. This includes our relationships at our work and place of business, school, or regular place of attendance, including those whom we see in our circle on a regular basis (such as grocers, gas station attendants, laundry folks, etc.). We can connect with these people because we share the same hobbies, recreation interests, share ethnic heritage, or national, or cultural associations.

Distinctives of Our Modern *Oikos* Networks

The nature of life today is dramatically different than that of the time of the apostles. In a culture where people are alienated greatly, and now largely connected with one another through digital media and platforms (e.g., Facebook, Twitter, "digital tribes," etc.), people connect anonymously through digital media, oftentimes with pseudonyms or under different guises. Despite the nature of digital connection, however, all human beings still belong to a distinctive *oikos* network where they are known, through which they relate, and in which they reside.

Truly, every urban person has an *oikos* of which they are a part. Of course, one's *oikos* connection in the city may not have anything (or very little) to do with *where the person is living*. As a rule, individuals are very suspicious and distrustful of people who are not a part of their *oikos* circle. Yet, once in a circle, one can find great friendship, companionship, and connections with others in their unique web of relationships.

What is perhaps most important in *oikos* web relationships is the idea that we tend to relate to people with whom we have connection, those who share in common with us, whether in kinship, interests, commitments, history, or experience. This is central to all human relating:

> As Christ had shared his life and his Spirit with them, they were free to share their life, money and goods with anyone who had need for them. "All the believers were one in heart and mind. No one claimed that any of [their] possessions was [their] own, but they shared everything they had" (Acts 4.32; see vv. 33–35). This movement of commonness was intimately connected to the apostles' presence and teaching, which had its roots in their life together as the Twelve and others with Jesus. The common life of Jesus with the Twelve became the common life of the apostles among the ecclesia, which became the common life of the ecclesia as household for any who had need, so "there were no needy persons among them."[27]

I can remember when I believed in the Good News of Christ for salvation. I was deeply involved in the drug culture, having made my living for some time through the sale of illicit drugs. After a time of soul searching and study (even for a brief turbulent stint with a friend and his Jehovah's Witnesses contacts), I discovered through reading a Barnes New Testament commentary on the Book of Revelation that Jesus of Nazareth was the Christ, the Son of God. It was the turning point of my life!

My first inclination to my new found faith was to go to my drug buddies and my family members and tell them of my new discovery. I took the only Bible I owned (my father's huge family Bible with pictures and places for family notes on marriage, kids, and what not!), visited my friends, and shared with them the news of my transformation, by belief in the Gospel, and its offer to them. It was poor evangelism strategy to share the Gospel to my druggie friends, while they smoked marijuana blunts and drank forty-ounce liquor bottles. They were not in either physical or spiritual condition to repent and believe.

To say the least, none showed interest in my new faith. As a matter of fact, one of them, Stephen, perhaps my dearest friend among them, expressed his discouragement with my change. He said something to the effect, "Don, I feel for you that you have become a Jesus freak. But, brotha', you wearin' us out! This is the last time I want you comin' 'roun' here sharing all that religious stuff. I'm sooner to believe in Batman and Robin than that. Just know, if you come around here sayin' that stuff again, me and the boys are going to put a whoop down on you. Period." I took this response as "No, I'm not interested in the Gospel!" I lost contact with him and the others for about a year.

Remarkably, a year or so later, my friend Stephen phoned me to apologize! He told me that he had not only repented and believed in Christ, but he had also accepted his call into Gospel ministry! Stephen and my friends were long-time drug dealers in the inner city. No well meaning, church going missionary was likely to go and tell them about Christ, nor would they have listened to them. But Stephen listened to me; we had lived together, sold drugs together, shared friends and lives together. And, when the Gospel touched my life, I could naturally share the Good News of Christ's offer to him.

As an ambassador for Christ, you must see your life (and all the relationships and connections which God has given to you) as avenues for you to provide clear and effective witness of Christ to those in your unique circle. Often we lament that we may not have been called to "full time ministry" as if the only valid spread of the Gospel is done through pastors, missionaries, and Christian workers.

Nothing could be further from the truth. God has called and gifted every disciple of Christ to use their time, treasure, and talent to share the Good News with those within their life circles, their unique family, friends, and associates. Every person who recognizes us, or whom we recognize, who "owns" us and is a "relative of ours" can be prayed for, related to, and witnessed to on behalf of Christ. If every believer were to pray, communicate, and share the Good News with those in their own circle, we could touch millions more people with the Gospel, and not hire a single "full-time worker" to join the cause!

Indeed, I am convinced that the key to winning those who do not know about our Lord will not be the recruitment of a new professional class of Christian workers, but the mobilization of ordinary disciples of Jesus to share with their friends, family members and associates where they live and work. This is the revolution we need, and the cause that we should seek!

Why We Should All Embrace *Oikos* Evangelism Today

I believe that we could transform ministry as we know it today if we could get our pretense on and simply affirm a basic, fundamental biblical truth related to Gospel ministry: *all Christians are called to share the hope of Christ with others, through the web of relationships that Christ has provided them today, now, in the place where he has placed them.* This truth is clearly given concisely and directly by the Apostle Peter in his first epistle:

> . . . but in your hearts honor Christ the Lord as holy, always being prepared to make a defense to anyone who asks you for a reason for the hope that is in you; yet do it with gentleness and respect, [16] having a good conscience, so that, when you are slandered, those who revile your good behavior in Christ may be put to shame.
>
> ~ 1 Peter 3.15-16

Every believer is called to make a defense to anyone who asks for a reason for the hope we have, and we must be prepared to give it, with gentleness and respect, with a good conscience and the kind of behavior that supports our claims. The challenge is given to all of us, every believer, every Christian recognizing their role as Christ's ambassador, and sharing the Good News with those with whom we relate.

What thrills me about this is simply every Christ follower, regardless of their status or station, can be *recruited to be a special agent of the Kingdom of God*, to touch the lives of the people in their *oikos*, where they live, play, and work. This means grammar school children, plumbers, teachers, secretaries, office workers, academics, lawyers, business folk, factory workers, grandmothers, retirees, and shop mechanics – literally everyone who names the name of Christ should be trained to share the Good News through their networks of family, friends, and associates! Can you imagine the impact of equipping literally millions to share the Gospel, in their circles, at their level, within their webs, all for the glory of Christ? We could transform our cities if we were to embrace this opportunity today.

There are great reasons to recruit, equip, and release believers of every age, level, and place to share the Good News within their relationship circles.

First, *oikos* evangelism is biblical. Jesus used household or *oikos* relationships to spread the Gospel regarding himself (e.g., Zaccheus, Luke 19.9; the Samaritan woman, John 4.53). Furthermore, the apostles ministered in this fashion (Peter with Cornelius, Acts 10-11; cf. Acts 10.24; Paul with Lydia and the Philippian jailer, Acts 16.12-15, 14-35). The *oikos* networks were not only the place for evangelism, but also where new Christians were discipled and gathered into congregations, cf. the households of Priscilla and Aquila, as well as Onesiphorus at Ephesus (1 Cor. 16.19; 2 Tim. 1.16; 2 Tim. 4.19).

Second, evidence suggests that most people come to faith in Christ through a member of their own relational network, their *oikos*. In a survey by Church Growth, Inc. of Monrovia, California, some 40,000 laypersons were polled as to how they entered into faith in Jesus Christ. The folk were given a simple basic question to answer: *"What or who was responsible for your coming to Jesus Christ and to your church?"* The respondents were to select one of eight possible answers:

(1) A "special need" brought them to Christ and the church.

(2) "Just walked in"

(3) "Pastor"

(4) "Visitation"

(5) "Sunday School"

(6) "Evangelistic crusade or television program"

(7) "Church program or outreach"

(8) "Friend or relative"

The results of the survey were incredible. Those who said special need was 1-2%, walk-ins were 2-3%, through a pastor 5-6%, by visitation 1-2%, through a Sunday School/small group kind of connection 4-5%, through an evangelistic crusade or TV show ½%, and a church outreach or program: 2-3%. However, those who said they came to faith through a friend or relatives was **75-90%**!

What a survey like this shows is the effectiveness of *oikos* connection when it comes to sharing the Good News with others. People are more inclined to listen to those whom they know, with whom they are connected, and in whom they trust.

Third, *oikos* members are already *receptive* to one another. This kind of evangelism builds on shared history, experience, and concerns. People of an *oikos* are more likely to listen to their own members than to strangers. The connection is there, the relationship already exists, cutting short the need for an evangelist, pastor, or church to cultivate a brand new relationship with them.

Fourth, *oikos* evangelism is built on *natural sharing* of the Gospel (*with no cold calling*). Barriers of culture, language, relationship melt away when members of an oikos share with other members of their group. It is the least threatening form of sharing faith or, for that matter, for receiving faith. Such sharing of the Lord occurs through normal relational lines. We are not relating to people as strangers, as "headhunters" alone, purely "targeting" people to proselytize them. Rather, no cold calling is involved in this kind of sharing. They are fellow students, co-workers, friends, family members, associates, people you know and those who know you. It is natural, simple, and open.[28]

Another benefit of this approach is that *oikos* evangelism greatly increases the number of *possible contacts* we can make with those who need to hear the Good News of Christ. In praying for, reaching out to, and witnessing with our *oikos* relationships, we are functioning in our own "built in," resident mission field. Our prayers for them (the very ground of effective evangelism) can be built on our understanding of their lives *specifically*, not of their needs *generically*. All those with whom an individual is associated become possible contacts for sharing the Good News. These contacts and folk will be relationally stronger for us, and for them. Rather than seeking to overcome a runaway culture of suspicion and mistrust, we can begin with our actual contacts with whom we relate day to day. *Oikos* relationships constantly re-seed a new contact base.

Sixth, *oikos* evangelism makes follow-up and connection with those who respond more likely and more natural. We are seeking to bring people into the Kingdom, to become active, fruitful members of the church, not mere abstract decision makers; we want them to become friends of God and of the church! *Oikos* evangelism makes connection and affiliation with other church members easier, and less strange or uncomfortable. Members of an *oikos, those whom already have connection and acquaintance,* can be established in the faith with people they already know and trust, turning from connections in the world to brothers and sisters in the faith (the entire book of Philemon is on this subject).

Finally, and perhaps most importantly, *oikos* evangelism *multiplies the number of laborers and workers* in the harvest field. Jesus declared that the harvest field is great, but the laborers are few. He exhorted us to ask the Lord of the harvest to send forth more laborers into the harvest field (Matt. 9.37-38). *Oikos* evangelism emphasizes the concept of "every disciple a minister" (Eph. 4.11-13), albeit not a clergy person or full-time Christian worker. Actually, our language is terrible on this point. Every disciple of Jesus is a full-time ambassador and laborer in the harvest *of their own unique, God-given oikos network*! Through the *oikos* emphasis, every believer who is growing in Christ can pray for the lost, share their testimony, win those who respond, and help establish new believers to share within their *oikos* (2 Tim. 2.2.). All of us can be mobilized to make a difference for Christ, right where we are, regardless of our age, vocation, place, station, or condition.

"Your Mission, If You Decide to Accept It: Live as Christ's Special Ambassador within Your *Oikos*"

In every episode of the hit TV series, *Mission: Impossible*, the IMF (Impossible Missions Force) were given details of an upcoming, possible mission, which always ended: "Your mission, if you decide to accept it, is to . . .(.)" They received the details and the facts, understood the stakes, and then had to accept the challenge of the mission. Once committed, he assembled the team, planned the operation, executed the mission, and completed the work – and each time with style, cleverness, and genius!

Truly, each of us is called to play our role in the story of God, to become members of the Kingdom of God and of the Church, forged with a new identity as free representatives of Christ, called to penetrate our circles with the Good News of the Savior.

God is not calling every Christian to serve as a clergyman, an evangelist, a church planter, or a missionary. He is calling each disciple to live out the meaning of the Gospel in the place where he has called them, with those whom they see, associate, and relate to. Your mission (and please, do accept it) is to represent Christ with honor in the place where he has placed you, among your family, friends, associates, and relationships.

Of course, there will be many in any given *oikos* who will simply not be open to the Gospel, and will repel the one who seeks to penetrate its ranks with it (Matt. 10.34-39 with Micah 7.6; Mark 13.12; Luke 21.16). We see too, in the Scriptures, if the Gospel is rejected by the leading members of an *oikos*, it may make it extremely difficult to continue to share within it. Those who are devoted to their *oikos* may even try to interfere with the new found allegiance of an *oikos* member to Jesus Christ (see John 12.42-43).

Regardless of the issues and challenges, you must begin to both *think and pray oikos*! The word *oikos* is related to our modern word "economics." Think "economically" in every personal relationship you make and cultivate. Make a list of the members of your *oikos*, and begin to pray by name and need for each one. Do not worry if you do not see the immediate impact of sowing seeds within your *oikos*. Simply pray for those in your *oikos*, sharing the Good News as God allows opportunity. In your planning and prayer, ask God to give you the entire circle! Pray for your friends, your family, and your associates. Pray for boldness to share with them, and ripe opportunities to draw attention to your hope in Christ. Become an Andrew to members of your *oikos* – remember, Andrew found Peter (John 1.40-42), and Philip found Nathanael (John 1.43-44). Expect God, the Holy Spirit, to move the message of the Good News naturally through the *oikos* relationships of the converts you see.

Conclusion

As ambassadors and agents of Jesus Christ, the *oikos* concept for evangelism and discipleship informs us how to proceed. We ought to pay careful attention to the *oikia* (plural of *oikos*) making up our neighborhoods. God has granted us the blessing of a web of common kinship relationships, friendships, and associations that make up our social circle. As the Spirit leads us, we can pray for and share the Good News with those in our network, and trust that God, through the power of that same Spirit, can spread the Gospel quickly along the lines of kinship, friendship, and association within it.

Who are those in your *oikos* network today? Of what family are you a part? Who are those neighbors and friends you know who need the Savior? What coworkers and associates do you know that need the love of God in their lives? Never forget the unique opportunity each disciple of Jesus has to pray for and witness to those kinfolk, friends, neighbors, and coworkers who belong to our *oikos*.

Now, let's pretend that you have been granted authority and power to represent the living Christ in the place where he has put you. Represent him with honor and courage. The Spirit will empower us to make disciples where we are, and salvation will come to those within our households, and beyond, all to the glory of God through Jesus Christ.

You are a kingdom citizen. You are Christ's ambassador. You've been called to represent him, and his Spirit will grant you the grace to do it with honor and excellence, if you so desire. Now, get your pretense on!

Appendices

Appendix 1

The Story of God: Our Sacred Roots

Rev. Dr. Don L. Davis

The Alpha and the Omega	Christus Victor	Come, Holy Spirit	Your Word Is Truth	The Great Confession	His Life in Us	Living in the Way	Reborn to Serve
The LORD God is the source, sustainer, and end of all things in the heavens and earth. All things were formed and exist by his will and for his eternal glory; the triune God, Father, Son, and Holy Spirit. Rom. 11.36.							
THE TRIUNE GOD'S UNFOLDING DRAMA — God's Self-Revelation in Creation, Israel, and Christ				THE CHURCH'S PARTICIPATION IN GOD'S UNFOLDING DRAMA — Fidelity to the Apostolic Witness to Christ and His Kingdom			
The Objective Foundation: The Sovereign Love of God — God's Narration of His Saving Work in Christ				The Subjective Practice: Salvation by Grace through Faith — The Redeemed's Joyous Response to God's Saving Work in Christ			
The Author of the Story	*The Champion of the Story*	*The Interpreter of the Story*	*The Testimony of the Story*	*The People of the Story*	*Re-enactment of the Story*	*Embodiment of the Story*	*Continuation of the Story*
The Father as *Director*	Jesus as *Lead Actor*	The Spirit as *Narrator*	Scripture as *Script*	As Saints, *Confessors*	As Worshipers, *Ministers*	As Followers, *Sojourners*	As Servants, *Ambassadors*
Christian *Worldview*	Communal *Identity*	Spiritual *Experience*	Biblical *Authority*	Orthodox *Theology*	Priestly *Worship*	Congregational *Discipleship*	Kingdom *Witness*
Theistic and Trinitarian Vision	Christ-centered Foundation	Spirit-indwelt and Filled Community	Canonical and Apostolic Witness	Ancient Creedal Affirmation of Faith	Weekly Gathering in Christian Assembly	Corporate, Ongoing Spiritual Formation	Active Agents of the Reign of God
Sovereign *Willing*	Messianic *Representing*	Divine *Comforting*	Inspired *Testifying*	Truthful *Retelling*	Joyful *Exceling*	Faithful *Indwelling*	Hopeful *Compelling*
Creator — True Maker of the Cosmos	Recapitulation — *Typos* and Fulfillment of the Covenant	Life-Giver — Regeneration and Adoption	Divine Inspiration — God-breathed Word	The Confession of Faith — Union with Christ	Song and Celebration — Historical Recitation	Pastoral Oversight — Shepherding the Flock	Explicit Unity — Love for the Saints
Owner — Sovereign Disposer of Creation	Revealer — Incarnation of the Word	Teacher — Illuminator of the Truth	Sacred History — Historical Record	Baptism into Christ — Communion of Saints	Homilies and Teachings — Prophetic Proclamation	Shared Spirituality — Common Journey through the Spiritual Disciplines	Radical Hospitality — Evidence of God's Kingdom Reign
Ruler — Blessed Controller of All Things	Redeemer — Reconciler of All Things	Helper — Endowment and the Power	Biblical Theology — Divine Commentary	The Rule of Faith — Apostles' Creed and Nicene Creed	The Lord's Supper — Dramatic Re-enactment	Embodiment — Anamnesis and Prolepsis through the Church Year	Extravagant Generosity — Good Works
Covenant Keeper — Faithful Promisor	Restorer — Christ, the Victor over the powers of evil	Guide — Divine Presence and Shekinah	Spiritual Food — Sustenance for the Journey	The Vincentian Canon — Ubiquity, antiquity, universality	Eschatological Foreshadowing — The Already/Not Yet	Effective Discipling — Spiritual Formation in the Believing Assembly	Evangelical Witness — Making Disciples of All People Groups

Appendix 2

A Call to an Ancient Evangelical Future

Robert Webber and Phil Kenyon, Northern Seminary

Revised 36 – May 5, 2006

Prologue

In every age the Holy Spirit calls the Church to examine its faithfulness to God's revelation in Jesus Christ, authoritatively recorded in Scripture and handed down through the Church. Thus, while we affirm the global strength and vitality of worldwide Evangelicalism in our day, we believe the North American expression of Evangelicalism needs to be especially sensitive to the new external and internal challenges facing God's people.

These external challenges include the current cultural milieu and the resurgence of religious and political ideologies. The internal challenges include Evangelical accommodation to civil religion, rationalism, privatism and pragmatism. In light of these challenges, we call Evangelicals to strengthen their witness through a recovery of the faith articulated by the consensus of the ancient Church and its guardians in the traditions of Eastern Orthodoxy, Roman Catholicism, the Protestant Reformation and the Evangelical awakenings. Ancient Christians faced a world of paganism, Gnosticism and political domination. In the face of heresy and persecution, they understood history through Israel's story, culminating in the death and resurrection of Jesus and the coming of God's Kingdom.

Today, as in the ancient era, the Church is confronted by a host of master narratives that contradict and compete with the gospel. The pressing question is: who gets to narrate the world? The *Call to an Ancient Evangelical Future* challenges Evangelical Christians to restore the priority of the divinely inspired biblical story of God's acts in history. The narrative of God's Kingdom holds eternal implications for the mission of the Church, its theological reflection, its public ministries of worship and spirituality and its life in the world. By engaging these themes, we believe the Church will be strengthened to address the issues of our day.

1. On the Primacy of the Biblical Narrative

We call for a return to the priority of the divinely authorized canonical story of the Triune God. This story – Creation, Incarnation, and Re-creation – was effected by Christ's recapitulation of human history and summarized by the early Church in its Rules of Faith. The gospel-formed content of these Rules served as the key to the interpretation of Scripture and its critique of contemporary culture, and thus shaped the church's pastoral ministry. Today, we call Evangelicals to turn away from modern theological methods that reduce the gospel to mere propositions, and from contemporary pastoral ministries so compatible with culture that they camouflage God's story or empty it of its cosmic and redemptive meaning. In a world of competing stories, we call Evangelicals to recover the truth of God's word as the story of the world, and to make it the centerpiece of Evangelical life.

2. On the Church, the Continuation of God's Narrative

We call Evangelicals to take seriously the visible character of the Church. We call for a commitment to its mission in the world in fidelity to God's mission (*Missio Dei*), and for an exploration of the ecumenical implications this has for the unity, holiness catholicity, and apostolicity of the Church. Thus, we call Evangelicals to turn away from an individualism that makes the Church a mere addendum to God's redemptive plan. Individualistic Evangelicalism has contributed to the current problems of churchless Christianity, redefinitions of the Church according to business models, separatist ecclesiologies and judgmental attitudes toward the Church. Therefore, we call Evangelicals to recover their place in the community of the Church catholic.

3. On the Church's Theological Reflection on God's Narrative

We call for the Church's reflection to remain anchored in the Scriptures in continuity with the theological interpretation learned from the early Fathers. Thus, we call Evangelicals to turn away from methods that separate theological reflection from the common traditions of the Church. These modern methods compartmentalize God's story by analyzing its separate parts, while ignoring God's entire redemptive work as recapitulated in Christ. Anti-historical attitudes also disregard the common biblical and theological legacy of the ancient Church. Such disregard ignores the hermeneutical value of the Church's ecumenical creeds. This reduces God's story of the world to one of many competing theologies and impairs the unified witness of the Church to God's plan for the history of the world. Therefore, we call Evangelicals to unity in "the tradition that has been believed everywhere, always and by all," as well as to humility and charity in their various Protestant traditions.

4. On Church's Worship as Telling and Enacting God's Narrative

We call for public worship that sings, preaches and enacts God's story. We call for a renewed consideration of how God ministers to us in baptism, eucharist, confession, the laying on of hands, marriage, healing and through the charisms of the Spirit, for these actions shape our lives and signify the meaning of the world. Thus, we call Evangelicals to turn away from forms of worship that focus on God as a mere object of the intellect, or that assert the self as the source of worship. Such worship has resulted in lecture-oriented, music-driven, performance-centered and program-controlled models that do not adequately proclaim God's cosmic redemption. Therefore, we call Evangelicals to recover the historic substance of worship of Word and Table and to attend to the Christian year, which marks time according to God's saving acts.

5. On Spiritual Formation in the Church as Embodiment of God's Narrative

We call for a catechetical spiritual formation of the people of God that is based firmly on a Trinitarian biblical narrative. We are concerned when spirituality is separated from the story of God and baptism into the life of Christ and his Body. Spirituality, made independent from God's story, is often characterized by legalism, mere intellectual knowledge, an overly therapeutic culture, New Age Gnosticism, a dualistic rejection of this world and a narcissistic preoccupation with one's own experience. These false spiritualities are inadequate for the challenges we face in today's world. Therefore, we call Evangelicals to return to a historic spirituality like that taught and practiced in the ancient catechumenate.

6. On the Church's Embodied Life in the World

We call for a cruciform holiness and commitment to God's mission in the world. This embodied holiness affirms life, biblical morality and appropriate self-denial. It calls us to be faithful stewards of the created order and bold prophets to our contemporary culture. Thus, we call Evangelicals to intensify their prophetic voice against forms of indifference to God's gift of life, economic and political injustice, ecological insensitivity and the failure to champion the poor and marginalized. Too often we have failed to stand prophetically against the culture's captivity to racism, consumerism, political correctness, civil religion, sexism, ethical relativism, violence and the culture of death. These failures have muted the voice of Christ to the world through his Church and detract from God's story of the world, which the Church is collectively to embody. Therefore, we call the Church to recover its counter-cultural mission to the world.

Epilogue

In sum, we call Evangelicals to recover the conviction that God's story shapes the mission of the Church to bear witness to God's Kingdom and to inform the spiritual foundations of civilization. We set forth this *Call* as an ongoing, open-ended conversation. We are aware that we have our blind spots and weaknesses. Therefore, we encourage Evangelicals to engage this *Call* within educational centers, denominations and local churches through publications and conferences.

We pray that we can move with intention to proclaim a loving, transcendent, triune God who has become involved in our history. In line with Scripture, creed and tradition, it is our deepest desire to embody God's purposes in the mission of the Church through our theological reflection, our worship, our spirituality and our life in the world, all the while proclaiming that Jesus is Lord over all creation.

Sponsors

Northern Seminary (www.seminary.edu)
Baker Books (www.bakerbooks.com)
Institute for Worship Studies (www.iwsfla.org)
InterVarsity Press (www.ivpress.com)

This *Call* is issued in the spirit of *sic et non*; therefore those who affix their names to this *Call* need not agree with all its content. Rather, its consensus is that these are issues to be discussed in the tradition of *semper reformanda* as the church faces the new challenges of our time. Over a period of seven months, more than 300 persons have participated via e-mail to write the *Call*. These men and women represent a broad diversity of ethnicity and denominational affiliation. The four theologians who most consistently interacted with the development of the *Call* have been named as *Theological Editors*. The *Board of Reference* was given the special assignment of overall approval.

If you wish to be a signer on the *Call* go to *www.ancientfutureworship.com.*

Appendix 3
The Nicene Creed with Biblical Support
The Urban Ministry Institute

We believe in one God, (Deut. 6.4-5; Mark 12.29; 1 Cor. 8.6)

the Father Almighty, (Gen. 17.1; Dan. 4.35; Matt. 6.9; Eph. 4.6; Rev. 1.8)

Maker of heaven and earth (Gen. 1.1; Isa. 40.28; Rev. 10.6)

and of all things visible and invisible. (Ps. 148; Rom. 11.36; Rev. 4.11)

We believe in one Lord Jesus Christ, the only Begotten Son of God, begotten of the Father before all ages, God from God, Light from Light, True God from True God, begotten not created, of the same essence as the Father,
(John 1.1-2; 3.18; 8.58; 14.9-10; 20.28; Col. 1.15, 17; Heb. 1.3-6)

through whom all things were made. (John 1.3; Col. 1.16)

Who for us men and for our salvation came down from heaven and was incarnate by the Holy Spirit and the Virgin Mary and became human. (Matt. 1.20-23; John 1.14; 6.38; Luke 19.10)

Who for us too, was crucified under Pontius Pilate, suffered and was buried.
(Matt. 27.1-2; Mark 15.24-39, 43-47; Acts 13.29; Rom. 5.8; Heb. 2.10; 13.12)

The third day he rose again according to the Scriptures,
(Mark 16.5-7; Luke 24.6-8; Acts 1.3; Rom. 6.9; 10.9; 2 Tim. 2.8)

ascended into heaven, and is seated at the right hand of the Father. (Mark 16.19; Eph. 1.19-20)

He will come again in glory to judge the living and the dead, and his Kingdom will have no end.
(Isa. 9.7; Matt. 24.30; John 5.22; Acts 1.11; 17.31; Rom. 14.9; 2 Cor. 5.10; 2 Tim. 4.1)

We believe in the Holy Spirit, the Lord and life-giver,

(Gen. 1.1-2; Job 33.4; Ps. 104.30; 139.7-8; Luke 4.18-19; John 3.5-6; Acts 1.1-2; 1 Cor. 2.11; Rev. 3.22)

who proceeds from the Father and the Son,

(John 14.16-18, 26; 15.26; 20.22)

who together with the Father and Son is worshiped and glorified,

(Isa. 6.3; Matt. 28.19; 2 Cor. 13.14; Rev. 4.8)

who spoke by the prophets.

(Num. 11.29; Mic. 3.8; Acts 2.17-18; 2 Pet. 1.21)

We believe in one holy, catholic, and apostolic Church.

(Matt. 16.18; Eph. 5.25-28; 1 Cor. 1.2; 10.17; 1 Tim. 3.15; Rev. 7.9)

We acknowledge one baptism for the forgiveness of sin,

(Acts 22.16; 1 Pet. 3.21; Eph. 4.4-5)

And we look for the resurrection of the dead and the life of the age to come.

(Isa. 11.6-10; Mic. 4.1-7; Luke 18.29-30; Rev. 21.1-5; 21.22-22.5)

Amen.

Memory Verses

Below are suggested memory verses, one for each section of the Creed.

The Father

Rev. 4.11 (ESV) – Worthy are you, our Lord and God, to receive glory and honor and power, for you created all things, and by your will they existed and were created.

The Son

John 1.1 (ESV) – In the beginning was the Word, and the Word was with God, and the Word was God.

The Son's Mission

1 Cor. 15.3-5 (ESV) – For what I received I passed on to you as of first importance: that Christ died for our sins according to the Scriptures, that he was buried, that he was raised on the third day according to the Scriptures, and that he appeared to Peter, and then to the Twelve.

The Holy Spirit

Rom. 8.11 (ESV) – If the Spirit of him who raised Jesus from the dead dwells in you, he who raised Christ Jesus from the dead will also give life to your mortal bodies through his Spirit who dwells in you.

The Church

1 Pet. 2.9 (ESV) – But you are a chosen race, a royal priesthood, a holy nation, a people for his own possession, that you may proclaim the excellencies of him who called you out of darkness into his marvelous light.

Our Hope

1 Thess. 4.16-17 (ESV) – For the Lord himself will descend from heaven with a cry of command, with the voice of an archangel, and with the sound of the trumpet of God. And the dead in Christ will rise first. Then we who are alive, who are left, will be caught up together with them in the clouds to meet the Lord in the air, and so we will always be with the Lord.

Appendix 4

Going Forward by Looking Back:
Toward an Evangelical Retrieval of the Great Tradition

Rev. Dr. Don L. Davis

Rediscovering the "Great Tradition"

In a wonderful little book, Ola Tjorhom,[1] describes the Great Tradition of the Church (sometimes called the "classical Christian tradition") as "living, organic, and dynamic."[2] The Great Tradition represents that evangelical, apostolic, and catholic core of Christian faith and practice which came largely to fruition from 100-500 AD.[3] Its rich legacy and treasures represent the Church's confession of what the Church has always believed, the worship that the ancient, undivided Church celebrated and embodied, and the mission that it embraced and undertook.

While the Great Tradition neither can substitute for the Apostolic Tradition (i.e., the authoritative source of all Christian faith, the Scriptures), nor should it overshadow the living presence of Christ in the Church through the Holy Spirit, it is still authoritative and

. . . .

1   Ola Tjorhom, *Visible Church–Visible Unity: Ecumenical Ecclesiology and "The Great Tradition of the Church."* Collegeville, Minnesota: Liturgical Press, 2004. Robert Webber defined the Great Tradition in this way: "[It is] the broad outline of Christian belief and practice developed from the Scriptures between the time of Christ and the middle of the fifth century." Robert E. Webber, *The Majestic Tapestry*. Nashville: Thomas Nelson Publishers, 1986, p. 10.

2   Ibid., p. 35.

3   The core of the Great Tradition concentrates on the formulations, confessions, and practices of the Church's first five centuries of life and work. Thomas Oden, in my judgment, rightly asserts that ". . . . most of what is enduringly valuable in contemporary biblical exegesis was discovered by the fifth century" (cf. Thomas C. Oden, *The Word of Life*. San Francisco: HarperSanFrancisco, 1989, p. xi.).

revitalizing for the people of God. It has and still can provide God's people through time with the substance of its confession and faith. The Great Tradition has been embraced and affirmed as authoritative by Catholic, Orthodox, Anglican, and Protestant theologians, those ancient and modern, as it has produced the seminal documents, doctrines, confessions, and practices of the Church (e.g., the canon of Scriptures, the doctrines of the Trinity, the deity of Christ, etc.).

Many evangelical scholars today believe that the way forward for dynamic faith and spiritual renewal will entail looking back, not with sentimental longings for the "good old days" of a pristine, problem-free early church, or a naive and even futile attempt to ape their heroic journey of faith. Rather, with a critical eye to history, a devout spirit of respect for the ancient Church, and a deep commitment to Scripture, we ought to rediscover through the Great Tradition the seeds of a new, authentic, and empowered faith. We can be transformed as we retrieve and are informed by the core beliefs and practices of the Church before the horrible divisions and fragmentations of Church history.

Well, if we do believe we ought to at least look again at the early Church and its life, or better yet, are convinced even to retrieve the Great Tradition for the sake of renewal in the Church – what exactly are we hoping to get back? Are we to uncritically accept everything the ancient Church said and did as "gospel," to be truthful simply because it is closer to the amazing events of Jesus of Nazareth in the world? Is old "hip," in and of itself?

No. We neither accept all things uncritically, nor do we believe that old, in and of itself, is truly good. Truth for us is more than ideas or ancient claims; for us, truth was incarnated in the person of Jesus of Nazareth, and the Scriptures give authoritative and final claim to the meaning of his revelation and salvation in history. We cannot accept things simply because they are reported to have been done in the past, or begun in the past. Amazingly, the Great Tradition itself argued for us to be critical, to contend for the faith once delivered to the saints (Jude 3), to embrace and celebrate the tradition received from the Apostles, rooted and interpreted by the Holy Scriptures themselves, and expressed in Christian confession and practice.

Core Dimensions of the Great Tradition

While Tjorhom offers his own list of ten elements of the theological content of the Great Tradition that he believes is worthy of reinterpretation and regard,[4] I believe there are seven dimensions that, from a biblical and spiritual vantage point, can enable us to understand what the early Church believed, how they worshiped and lived, and the ways they defended their living faith in Jesus Christ. Through their allegiance to the documents, confessions, and practices of this period, the ancient Church bore witness to God's salvation promise in the midst of a pagan and crooked generation. The core of our current faith and practice was developed in this era, and deserves a second (and twenty-second) look.

Adapting, redacting, and extending Tjorhom's notions of the Great Tradition, I list here what I take to be, as a start, a simple listing of the critical dimensions that deserve our undivided attention and wholehearted retrieval.

1. *The Apostolic Tradition.* The Great Tradition is rooted in the Apostolic Tradition, i.e., the apostles' eyewitness testimony

. . . .

4   Ibid., pp. 27-29. Tjorhom's ten elements are argued in the context of his work where he also argues for the structural elements and the ecumenical implications of retrieving the Great Tradition. I wholeheartedly agree with the general thrust of his argument, which, like my own belief, makes the claim that an interest in and study of the Great Tradition can renew and enrich the contemporary Church in its worship, service, and mission.

and firsthand experience of Jesus of Nazareth, their authoritative witness to his life and work recounted in the Holy Scriptures, the canon of our Bible today. The Church is apostolic, built on the foundation of the prophets and the apostles, with Christ himself being the Cornerstone. The Scriptures themselves represent the source of our interpretation about the Kingdom of God, that story of God's redemptive love embodied in the promise to Abraham and the patriarchs, in the covenants and experience of Israel, and which culminates in the revelation of God in Christ Jesus, as predicted in the prophets and explicated in the apostolic testimony.

2. ***The Ecumenical Councils and Creeds, Especially the Nicene Creed.*** The Great Tradition declares the truth and sets the bounds of the historic orthodox faith as defined and asserted in the ecumenical creeds of the ancient and undivided Church, with special focus on the Nicene Creed. Their declarations were taken to be an accurate interpretation and commentary on the teachings of the apostles set in Scripture. While not the *source* of the Faith itself, the confession of the ecumenical councils and creeds represents the *substance of its teachings*,[5] especially those before the fifth century (where virtually all of the elemental doctrines concerning God, Christ, and salvation were articulated and embraced).[6]

· ·

5   I am indebted to the late Dr. Robert E. Webber for this helpful distinction between the source and the substance of Christian faith and interpretation.

6   While the seven ecumenical Councils (along with others) are affirmed by both Catholic and Orthodox communions as binding, it is the first four Councils that are to be considered the critical, most essential confessions of the ancient, undivided Church. I and others argue for this largely because the first four articulate and settle once and for all what is to be considered our orthodox faith on the doctrines of the Trinity and the Incarnation (cf. Philip Schaff, *The Creeds of Christendom*, v. 1. Grand Rapids: Baker Book House,

3. *The Ancient Rule of Faith.* The Great Tradition embraced the substance of this core Christian faith in a rule, i.e., an ancient standard rule of faith, that was considered to be the yardstick by which claims and propositions regarding the interpretation of the biblical faith were to be assessed. This rule, when applied reverently and rigorously, can clearly allow us to define the core Christian confession of the ancient and undivided Church expressed clearly in that instruction and adage of Vincent of Lerins: "that which has always been believed, everywhere, and by all."[7]

4. *The Christus Victor Worldview.* The Great Tradition celebrates and affirms Jesus of Nazareth as the Christ, the promised

. . . .

1996, p. 44). Similarly, even the magisterial Reformers embraced the teaching of the Great Tradition, and held its most significant confessions as authoritative. Correspondingly, Calvin could argue in his own theological interpretations that "Thus councils would come to have the majesty that is their due; yet in the meantime Scripture would stand out in the higher place, with everything subject to its standard. In this way, we willingly embrace and reverence as holy the early councils, such as those of Nicea, Constantinople, the first of Ephesus I, Chalcedon, and the like, which were concerned with refuting errors – in so far as they relate to the teachings of faith. For they contain nothing but the pure and genuine exposition of Scripture, which the holy Fathers applied with spiritual prudence to crush the enemies of religion who had then arisen" (cf. John Calvin, *Institutes of the Christian Religion*, IV, ix. 8. John T. McNeill, ed. Ford Lewis Battles, trans. Philadelphia: Westminster Press, 1960, pp. 1171-72).

7   This rule, which has won well-deserved favor down through the years as a sound theological yardstick for authentic Christian truth, weaves three cords of critical assessment to determine what may be counted as orthodox or not in the Church's teaching. St. Vincent of Lerins, a theological commentator who died before 450 AD, authored what has come to be called the "Vincentian canon, a three-fold test of catholicity: *quod ubique, quod semper, quod ab omnibus creditum est* (what has been believed everywhere, always and by all). By this three-fold test of ecumenicity, antiquity, and consent, the church may discern between true and false traditions." (cf. Thomas C. Oden, *Classical Pastoral Care*, vol. 4. Grand Rapids: Baker Books, 1987, p. 243).

Messiah of the Hebrew Scriptures, the risen and exalted Lord, and Head of the Church. In Jesus of Nazareth alone, God has reasserted his reign over the universe, having destroyed death in his dying, conquering God's enemies through his incarnation, death, resurrection, and ascension, and ransoming humanity from its penalty due to its transgression of the Law. Now resurrected from the dead, ascended and exalted at the right hand of God, he has sent the Holy Spirit into the world to empower the Church in its life and witness. The Church is to be considered the people of the victory of Christ. At his return, he will consummate his work as Lord. This worldview was expressed in the ancient Church's confession, preaching, worship, and witness. Today, through its liturgy and practice of the Church Year, the Church acknowledges, celebrates, embodies, and proclaims this victory of Christ: the destruction of sin and evil and the restoration of all creation.

5. *The Centrality of the Church.* The Great Tradition confidently confessed the Church as the people of God. The faithful assembly of believers, under the authority of the Shepherd Christ Jesus, is now the locus and agent of the Kingdom of God on earth. In its worship, fellowship, teaching, service, and witness, Christ continues to live and move. The Great Tradition insists that the Church, under the authority of its undershepherds and the entirety of the priesthood of believers, is visibly the dwelling of God in the Spirit in the world today. With Christ himself being the Chief Cornerstone, the Church is the temple of God, the body of Christ, and the temple of the Holy Spirit. All believers, living, dead, and yet unborn – make up the one, holy, catholic (universal), and apostolic community. Gathering together regularly in believing assembly, members of the Church meet locally to worship God through Word and sacrament, and to bear witness in its good works and proclamation of the Gospel. Incorporating new believers

into the Church through baptism, the Church embodies the
life of the Kingdom in its fellowship, and demonstrates in
word and deed the reality of the Kingdom of God through its
life together and service to the world.

6. *The Unity of the Faith.* The Great Tradition affirms
   unequivocally the catholicity of the Church of Jesus Christ,
   in that it is concerned with keeping communion and
   continuity with the worship and theology of the Church
   throughout the ages (Church universal). Since there has
   been and can only be one hope, calling, and faith, the Great
   Tradition fought and strove for oneness in word, in doctrine,
   in worship, in charity.

7. *The Evangelical Mandate of the Risen Christ.* The Great
   Tradition affirms the apostolic mandate to make known to
   the nations the victory of God in Jesus Christ, proclaiming
   salvation by grace through faith in his name, and inviting all
   peoples to repentance and faith to enter into the Kingdom of
   God. Through acts of justice and righteousness, the Church
   displays the life of the Kingdom in the world today, and through
   its preaching and life together provides a witness and sign of
   the Kingdom present in and for the world (*sacramentum
   mundi*), and as the pillar and ground of the truth. As evidence
   of the Kingdom of God and custodians of the Word of God,
   the Church is charged to define clearly and defend the faith
   once for all delivered to the Church by the apostles.

Conclusion: Finding Our Future by Looking Back

In a time where so many are confused by the noisy chaos of so
many claiming to speak for God, it is high time for us to rediscover
the roots of our faith, to go back to the beginning of Christian
confession and practice, and see, if in fact, we can recover our
identity in the stream of Christ worship and discipleship that

changed the world. In my judgment, this can be done through a critical, evangelical appropriation of the Great Tradition, that core belief and practice which is the source of all our traditions, whether Catholic, Orthodox, Anglican, or Protestant.

Of course, specific traditions will continue to seek to express and live out their commitment to the Authoritative Tradition (i.e., the Scriptures) and Great Tradition through their worship, teaching, and service. Our diverse Christian traditions (little "t"), when they are rooted in and expressive of the teaching of Scripture and led by the Holy Spirit, will continue to make the Gospel clear within new cultures or sub-cultures, speaking and modeling the hope of Christ into new situations shaped by their own set of questions posed in light of their own unique circumstances. Our traditions are essentially movements of contextualization, that is they are attempts to make plain within people groups the Authoritative Tradition in a way that faithfully and effectively leads them to faith in Jesus Christ.

We ought, therefore, to find ways to enrich our contemporary traditions by reconnecting and integrating our contemporary confessions and practices with the Great Tradition. Let us never forget that Christianity, at its core, is a faithful witness to God's saving acts in history. As such, we will always be a people who seek to find our futures by looking back through time at those moments of revelation and action where the Rule of God was made plain through the incarnation, passion, resurrection, ascension, and soon-coming of Christ. Let us then remember, celebrate, reenact, learn afresh, and passionately proclaim what believers have confessed since the morning of the empty tomb – the saving story of God's promise in Jesus of Nazareth to redeem and save a people for his own.

Appendix 5

Jesus of Nazareth: The Presence of the Future

Rev. Dr. Don L. Davis

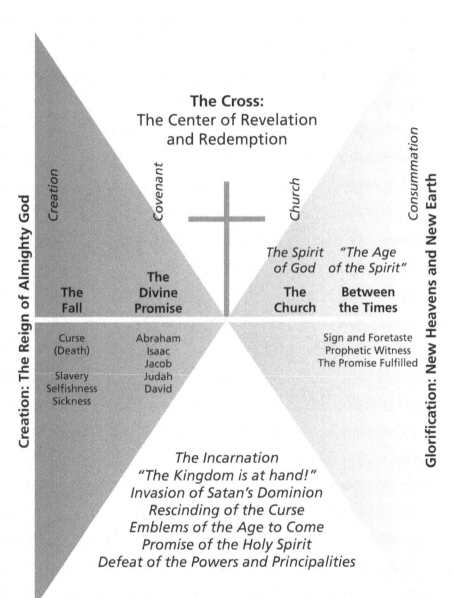

Appendix 6

The Theology of Christus Victor

Rev. Dr. Don L. Davis

	The Promised Messiah	The Word Made Flesh	The Son of Man	The Suffering Servant	The Lamb of God	The Victorious Conqueror	The Reigning Lord in Heaven	The Bridegroom and Coming King
Biblical Framework	Israel's hope of Yahweh's anointed who would redeem his people	In the person of Jesus of Nazareth, the Lord has come to the world	As the promised king and divine Son of Man, Jesus reveals the Father's glory and salvation to the world	As Inaugurator of the Kingdom of God, Jesus demonstrates God's reign present through his words, wonders, and works	As both High Priest and Paschal Lamb, Jesus offers himself to God on our behalf as a sacrifice for sin	In his resurrection from the dead and ascension to God's right hand, Jesus is proclaimed as Victor over the power of sin and death	Now reigning at God's right hand till his enemies are made his footstool, Jesus pours out his benefits on his body	Soon the risen and ascended Lord will return to gather his Bride, the Church, and consummate his work
Scripture References	Isa. 9.6-7 Jer. 23.5-6 Isa. 11.1-10	John 1.14-18 Matt. 1.20-23 Phil. 2.6-8	Matt. 2.1-11 Num. 24.17 Luke 1.78-79	Mark 1.14-15 Matt. 12.25-30 Luke 17.20-21	2 Cor. 5.18-21 Isa. 52-53 John 1.29	Eph. 1.16-23 Phil. 2.5-11 Col. 1.15-20	1 Cor. 15.25 Eph. 4.15-16 Acts 2.32-36	Rom. 14.7-9 Rev. 5.9-13 1 Thess. 4.13-18
Jesus' History	The pre-incarnate, only begotten Son of God in glory	His conception by the Spirit, and birth to Mary	His manifestation to the Magi and to the world	His teaching, exorcisms, miracles, and mighty works among the people	His suffering, crucifixion, death, and burial	His resurrection, with appearances to his witnesses, and his ascension to the Father	The sending of the Holy Spirit and his gifts, and Christ's session in heaven at the Father's right hand	His soon return from heaven to earth as Lord and Christ: the Second Coming
Description	The biblical promise for the seed of Abraham, the prophet like Moses, the son of David	In the Incarnation, God has come to us; Jesus reveals to humankind the Father's glory in fullness	In Jesus, God has shown his salvation to the entire world, including the Gentiles	In Jesus, the promised Kingdom of God has come visibly to earth, demonstrating his binding of Satan and rescinding the Curse	As God's perfect Lamb, Jesus offers himself up to God as a sin offering on behalf of the entire world	In his resurrection and ascension, Jesus destroyed death, disarmed Satan, and rescinded the Curse	Jesus is installed at the Father's right hand as Head of the Church, Firstborn from the dead, and supreme Lord in heaven	As we labor in his harvest field in the world, so we await Christ's return, the fulfillment of his promise
Church Year	Advent	Christmas	Season after Epiphany Baptism and Transfiguration	Lent	Holy Week Passion	Eastertide Easter, Ascension Day, Pentecost	Season after Pentecost Trinity Sunday	Season after Pentecost All Saints Day, Reign of Christ the King
	The Coming of Christ	*The Birth of Christ*	*The Manifestation of Christ*	*The Ministry of Christ*	*The Suffering and Death of Christ*	*The Resurrection and Ascension of Christ*	*The Heavenly Session of Christ*	*The Reign of Christ*
Spiritual Formation	As we await his Coming, let us proclaim and affirm the hope of Christ	O Word made flesh, let us every heart prepare him room to dwell	Divine Son of Man, show the nations your salvation and glory	In the person of Christ, the power of the reign of God has come to earth and to the Church	May those who share the Lord's death be resurrected with him	Let us participate by faith in the victory of Christ over the power of sin, Satan, and death	Come, indwell us, Holy Spirit, and empower us to advance Christ's Kingdom in the world	We live and work in expectation of his soon return, seeking to please him in all things

Appendix 7

Substitute Centers to a Christ-Centered Vision:
Goods and Effects Which Our Culture Substitutes as the Ultimate Concern

Rev. Dr. Don L. Davis

Christianity as allegiance to the person of **Jesus of Nazareth**

Christianity as Doctrine and Theology

Christianity as Ethics, Decency, and Middle-class Morality

Christianity as Patriotism, Political Vision, and Family Fulfillment

Christianity as Distinctly Western Religion (as opposed to the Eastern or other religious faiths)

Christianity as Personal Growth and Improvement

Christianity as Marriage Fulfillment and Family Development

Christianity as Benevolence, Alms, and Social Justice

Christianity as Pursuit of Prosperity and Blessing

Appendix 8

Our Declaration of Dependence: Freedom in Christ

Rev. Dr. Don L. Davis

It is important to teach Christian morality within the realm of the freedom that was won for us by Christ's death on the Cross, and the entrance of the Holy Spirit into the life and mission of the Church (i.e., Galatians 5.1, "It is for freedom Christ has set you free"), and always in the context of using your freedom in the framework of bringing God glory and advancing Christ's Kingdom. Along with some critical texts on freedom in the Epistles, I believe we can equip others to live for Christ and his Kingdom by emphasizing the "6-8-10" principles of 1 Corinthians, and apply them to all moral issues.

1. 1 Cor. 6.9-11 – Christianity is about transformation in Christ; no amount of excuses will get a person into the Kingdom.

2. 1 Cor. 6.12a – We are free in Christ, but not everything one does is edifying or helpful.

3. 1 Cor. 6.12b – We are free in Christ, but anything that is addictive and exercising control over you is counter to Christ and his Kingdom.

4. 1 Cor. 8.7-13 – We are free in Christ, but we ought never to flaunt our freedom, especially in the face of Christians whose conscience would be marred and who would stumble if they see us doing something they find offensive.

5. 1 Cor. 10.23 – We are free in Christ; all things are lawful for us, but not everything is helpful, nor does doing everything build oneself up.

6. 1 Cor. 10.24 – We are free in Christ, and ought to use our freedom to love our brothers and sisters in Christ, and nurture them for others' well being (cf. Gal. 5.13).

7. 1 Cor. 10.31 – We are free in Christ, and are given that freedom in order that we might glorify God in all that we do, whether we eat or drink, or anything else we do.

8. 1 Cor. 10.32-33 – We are free in Christ, and ought to use our freedom in order to do what we can to give no offense to people in the world or the Church, but do what we do in order to influence them to know and love Christ, i.e., that they might be saved.

In addition to these principles, I believe we ought also to emphasize the following principles:

- 1 Pet. 2.16 – We ought to live free in Christ as servants of God, but never seek to use our freedom as a cover-up for evil.

- John 8.31-32 – We show ourselves to be disciples of Christ as we abide and continue in his Word, and in so doing we come to know the truth, and the truth sets us free in him.

- Gal. 5.13 – As brothers and sisters in Christ, we are called to be free, yet not to use our freedom as a license to indulge our sinful natures; rather, we are called to be free in order to serve one another in love.

This focus on freedom, in my mind, places all things that we say to adults or teens in context. Often, the way in which we disciple many new Christians is through a rigorous taxonomy (listing) of different vices and moral ills, and this can, at times, not only give them the sense that Christianity is an anti-act religion (a religion of simply not doing things), and/or a faith overly concerned with not sinning. Actually, the moral focus in Christianity is on freedom, a freedom won at high price, a freedom to love God and advance the Kingdom, a freedom to live a surrendered life before the Lord. The moral responsibility of urban Christians is to live free in Jesus Christ, to live free unto God's glory, and to not use their freedom from the law as a license for sin.

The core of the teaching, then, is to focus on the freedom won for us through Christ's death and resurrection, and our union with him. We are now set free from the law, the principle of sin and death, the condemnation and guilt of our own sin, and the conviction of the law on us. We serve God now out of gratitude and thankfulness, and the moral impulse is living free in Christ. Yet, we do not use our freedom to be wiseguys or knuckle-heads, but to glorify God and love others. This is the context that addresses the thorny issues of homosexuality, abortion, and other social ills. Those who engage in such acts feign freedom, but, lacking a knowledge of God in Christ, they are merely following their own internal predispositions, which are not informed either by God's moral will or his love.

Freedom in Christ is a banner call to live holy and joyously as urban disciples. This freedom will enable them to see how creative they can be as Christians in the midst of so-called "free" living which only leads to bondage, shame, and remorse.

Appendix 9

Thirty-three Blessings in Christ

Rev. Dr. Don L. Davis

Did you know that thirty-three things happened to you at the moment you became a believer in Jesus Christ? Lewis Sperry Chafer, the first president of Dallas Theological Seminary, listed these benefits of salvation in his *Systematic Theology, Volume III* (pp. 234-266). These points, along with brief explanations, give the born-again Christian a better understanding of the work of grace accomplished in his/her life as well as a greater appreciation of his/her new life.

1. In the eternal plan of God, the believer is:

    a. *Foreknown* – Acts 2.23; 1 Pet. 1.2, 20. God knew from all eternity every step in the entire program of the universe.

    b. *Predestined* – Rom. 8.29-30. A believer's destiny has been appointed through foreknowledge to the unending realization of all God's riches of grace.

    c. *Elected* – Rom. 8.38; Col. 3.12. He/she is chosen of God in the present age and will manifest the grace of God in future ages.

    d. *Chosen* – Eph. 1.4. God has separated unto himself his elect who are both foreknown and predestined.

    e. *Called* – 1 Thess. 6.24. God invites man to enjoy the benefits of his redemptive purposes. This term may include those whom God has selected for salvation, but who are still in their unregenerate state.

2. A believer has been *redeemed* – Rom. 3.24. The price required to set him/her free from sin has been paid.

3. A believer has been *reconciled* – 2 Cor. 6.18, 19; Rom. 5.10. He/she is both restored to fellowship by God and restored to fellowship with God.

4. A believer is related to God through *propitiation* – Rom. 3.24-26. He/she has been set free from judgment by God's satisfaction with his Son's death for sinners.

5. A believer has been *forgiven* all trespasses – Eph. 1.7. All his/her sins are taken care of – past, present, and future.

6. A believer is vitally *conjoined to Christ* for the judgment of the old man "unto a new walk" – Rom. 6.1-10. He/she is brought into a union with Christ.

7. A believer is *"free from the law"* – Rom. 7.2-6. He/she is both dead to its condemnation, and delivered from its jurisdiction.

8. A believer has been made a *child of God* – Gal. 3.26. He/she is born anew by the regenerating power of the Holy Spirit into a relationship in which God the First Person becomes a legitimate Father and the saved one becomes a legitimate child with every right and title – an heir of God and a joint heir with Jesus Christ.

9. A believer has been *adopted as an adult child* into the Father's household – Rom. 8.15, 23.

10. A believer has been *made acceptable to God* by Jesus Christ – Eph. 1.6. He/she is made *righteous* (Rom. 3.22), *sanctified*

(set apart) positionally (1 Cor. 1.30, 6.11); *perfected forever in his/her standing and position* (Heb. 10.14), and *made acceptable* in the Beloved (Col. 1.12).

11. A believer has been *justified* – Rom. 5.1. He/she has been declared righteous by God's decree.

12. A believer is *"made right"* – Eph. 2.13. A close relation is set up and exists between God and the believer.

13. A believer has been *delivered from the power of darkness* – Col. 1.13; 2.13. A Christian has been delivered from Satan and his evil spirits. Yet the disciple must continue to wage warfare against these powers.

14. A believer has been *translated into the Kingdom of God* – Col. 1.13. The Christian has been transferred from Satan's kingdom to Christ's Kingdom.

15. A believer is *planted* on the Rock, Jesus Christ – 1 Cor. 3.9-15. Christ is the foundation on which the believer stands and on which he/she builds his/her Christian life.

16. A believer is a *gift from God to Jesus Christ* – John 17.6, 11, 12, 20. He/she is the Father's love gift to Jesus Christ.

17. A believer is *circumcised in Christ* – Col. 2.11. He/she has been delivered from the power of the old sin nature.

18. A believer has been made a *partaker of the Holy and Royal Priesthood* – 1 Pet. 2.5, 9. He/she is a priest because of his/her relation to Christ, the High Priest, and will reign on earth with Christ.

19. A believer is part of a *chosen generation, a holy nation and a peculiar people* – 1 Pet. 2.9. This is the company of believers in this age.

20. A believer is a *heavenly citizen* – Phil. 3.20. Therefore he/she is called a stranger as far as his/her life on earth is concerned (1 Pet. 2.13), and will enjoy his/her true home in heaven forever.

21. A believer is in *the family and household of God* – Eph. 2.1, 9. He/she is part of God's "family" which is composed only of true believers.

22. A believer is in *the fellowship of the saints* – John 17.11, 21-23. He/she can be a part of the fellowship of believers with one another.

23. A believer is in *a heavenly association* – Col. 1.27; 3.1; 2 Cor. 6.1; Col. 1.24; John 14.12-14; Eph. 5.25-27; Titus 2.13. He/she is a partner with Christ now in life, position, service, suffering, prayer, betrothal as a bride to Christ, and expectation of the coming again of Christ.

24. A believer has *access to God* – Eph. 2.18. He/she has access to God's grace which enables him/her to grow spiritually, and he/she has unhindered approach to the Father (Heb. 4.16).

25. A believer is within *the "much more" care of God* – Rom. 5.8-10. He/she is an object of God's love (John 3.16), God's grace (Eph. 2.7-9), God's power (Eph. 1.19), God's faithfulness (Phil. 1.6), God's peace (Rom. 5.1), God's consolation (2 Thess. 2.16-17), and God's intercession (Rom. 8.26).

26. A believer is *God's inheritance* – Eph. 1.18. He/she is given to Christ as a gift from the Father.

27. A believer *has the inheritance of God himself* and all that God bestows – 1 Pet. 1.4.

28. A believer has *light in the Lord* – 2 Cor. 4.6. He/she not only has this light, but is commanded to walk in the light.

29. A believer is *vitally united to the Father, the Son and the Holy Spirit* – 1 Thess. 1.1; Eph. 4.6; Rom. 8.1; John 14.20; Rom. 8.9; 1 Cor. 2.12.

30. A believer is blessed with *the earnest or firstfruits of the Spirit* – Eph. 1.14; 8.23. He/she is born of the Spirit (John 3.6), and baptized by the Spirit (1 Cor. 12.13), which is a work of the Holy Spirit by which the believer is joined to Christ's body and comes to be "in Christ," and therefore is a partaker of all that Christ is. The disciple is also indwelt by the Spirit (Rom. 8.9), sealed by the Spirit (2 Cor. 1.22), making him/her eternally secure, and filled with the Spirit (Eph. 5.18) whose ministry releases his power and effectiveness in the heart in which he dwells.

31. A believer is *glorified* – Rom. 8.18. He/she will be a partaker of the infinite story of the Godhead.

32. A believer is *complete in God* – Col. 2.9, 10. He/she partakes of all that Christ is.

33. A believer *possesses every spiritual blessing* – Eph. 1.3. All the riches tabulated in the other 32 points made before are to be included in this sweeping term, "all spiritual blessings."

It would hardly be amiss to restate the truth that salvation is a work of God for man and not a work for God. It is what God's love prompts him to do and not a mere act of pity which rescues creatures from their misery. To realize the satisfaction of his love,

God has been willing to remove by an infinite sacrifice the otherwise insuperable hindrance which sin has imposed; he is, likewise, overcoming the wicked opposition to his grace which the fallen human will presents by inclining his elect ones to exercise saving faith in Christ. When the way is thus clear, God is free to do all that infinite love dictates. Nothing short of transformations which are infinite will satisfy infinite love. An inadequate record of these riches of grace which together represent the infinity of saving grace has been submitted; but it still remains true that "the half has never been told." The student who is ambitious to be accurate in gospel preaching will not only observe but ever contend for the truth that all these riches are purely a work of God, and that to secure them the individual could do no more than to receive at the hand of God what he is free to give in and through Christ Jesus. Those who believe on Christ in the sense that they receive him (John 1.12) as their Savior enter instantly into all that divine love provides. These thirty-three positions and possessions are not bestowed in succession, but simultaneously. They do not require a period of time for their execution; but are wrought instantaneously. They measure the present difference which obtains between one who is saved and one who is not saved.

> Oh to grace how great a debtor
> Daily I'm constrained to be!
> Let Thy goodness, like a fetter,
> Bind my wandering heart to Thee.

Appendix 10

Ethics of the New Testament:
Living in the Upside-Down Kingdom of God

Rev. Dr. Don L. Davis

The Principle of Reversal

The Principle Expressed	Scripture
The poor shall become rich, and the rich shall become poor	Luke 6.20-26
The law breaker and the undeserving are saved	Matt. 21.31-32
Those who humble themselves shall be exalted	1 Pet. 5.5-6
Those who exalt themselves shall be brought low	Luke 18.14
The blind shall be given sight	John 9.39
Those claiming to see shall be made blind	John 9.40-41
We become free by being Christ's slave	Rom. 12.1-2
God has chosen what is foolish in the world to shame the wise	1 Cor. 1.27
God has chosen what is weak in the world to shame the strong	1 Cor. 1.27
God has chosen the low and despised to bring to nothing things that are	1 Cor. 1.28
We gain the next world by losing this one	1 Tim. 6.7
Love this life and you'll lose it; hate this life, and you'll keep the next	John 12.25

The Principle Expressed	Scripture
You become the greatest by being the servant of all	Matt. 10.42-45
Store up treasures here, you forfeit heaven's reward	Matt. 6.19
Store up treasures above, you gain heaven's wealth	Matt. 6.20
Accept your own death to yourself in order to live fully	John 12.24
Release all earthly reputation to gain heaven's favor	Phil. 3.3-7
The first shall be last, and the last shall become first	Mark 9.35
The grace of Jesus is perfected in your weakness, not your strength	2 Cor. 12.9
God's highest sacrifice is contrition and brokenness	Ps. 51.17
It is better to give to others than to receive from them	Acts 20.35
Give away all you have in order to receive God's best	Luke 6.38

Appendix 11

Laws of Sowing and Reaping

Rev. Dr. Don L. Davis

The Laws of Sowing and Reaping: Personal Discipline and Fruitfulness	
The Law	**The Explanation**
You will reap what you sow	Sow to the Spirit and reap God's best
You will reap what others have sown	Transcend the harvest you have inherited
You reap the same in kind as what you sow	Choose wisely what you want to reap before you sow
You reap in proportion to what you sow	Sow more to get more in return
You reap in a different season than when you sow	Learn to be patient as you await the harvest
You reap more than what you sow	It is going to be better (or worse) than you gave
You can always transcend last year's harvest	God gives the growth, so trust in him alone

We cannot help but see that the [people] who have achieved wonders in modern science and technology are [people] of very great inner discipline. No one has succeeded by following the path of least resistance.

~ Elton Trueblood. *The Yoke of Christ.*
Waco, TX: Word Books, 1958. p. 128.

Prayer and Affirmation to God

Do not be deceived: God is not mocked, for whatever one sows, that will he also reap. [8] For the one who sows to his own flesh will from the flesh reap corruption, but the one who sows to the Spirit will from the Spirit reap eternal life. [9] And let us not grow weary of doing good, for in due season we will reap, if we do not give up.

~ Galatians 6.7-9

Appendix 12

The Hump

Rev. Dr. Don L. Davis

The Baby Christian
The New Believer and the Spiritual Disciplines

Awkwardness

Unskillfulness

Mistakes

Roughness

Sporadic Behavior

Uncomfortableness

Inefficiency

Novice-Level Performance

The Mature Christian
The Mature Believer and the Spiritual Disciplines

Faithful Application

Gracefulness

Automatic response

Comfortableness

Personal Satisfaction

Excellence

Expertise

Training Others

Heart Desire
A Clear Goal
Feasible Plan
Solid Support
Correct Knowledge
Faithful Effort
Good Examples
Extended Period of Time
Longsuffering

Regular, correct application of the spiritual disciplines

Appendix 13

From Deep Ignorance to Credible Witness

Rev. Dr. Don L. Davis

Witness - Ability to give witness and teach
2 Tim. 2.2
Matt. 28.18-20
1 John 1.1-4
Prov. 20.6
2 Cor. 5.18-21

And the things you have heard me say in the presence of many witnesses entrust to reliable men who will also be qualified to teach others.
~ 2 Tim. 2.2

8

Lifestyle - Consistent appropriation and habitual practice based on beliefs
Heb. 5.11-6.2
Eph. 4.11-16
2 Pet. 3.18
1 Tim. 4.7-10

And Jesus increased in wisdom and in stature, and in favor with God and man.
~ Luke 2.52

7

Demonstration - Expressing conviction in corresponding conduct, speech, and behavior
James 2.14-26
2 Cor. 4.13
2 Pet. 1.5-9
1 Thess. 1.3-10

Nevertheless, at your word I will let down the net.
~ Luke 5.5

6

Conviction - Committing oneself to think, speak, and act in light of information
Heb. 2.3-4
Heb. 11.1, 6
Heb. 3.15-19
Heb. 4.2-6

Do you believe this?
~ John 11.26

5

Discernment - Understanding the meaning and implications of information
John 16.13
Eph. 1.15-18
Col. 1.9-10
Isa. 6.10; 29.10

Do you understand what you are reading?
~ Acts 8.30

4

Knowledge - Ability to recall and recite information
2 Tim. 3.16-17
1 Cor. 2.9-16
1 John 2.20-27
John 14.26

For what does the Scripture say?
~ Rom. 4.3

3

Interest - Responding to ideas or information with both curiosity and openness
Ps. 42.1-2
Acts 9.4-5
John 12.21
1 Sam. 3.4-10

We will hear you again on this matter.
~ Acts 17.32

2

Awareness - General exposure to ideas and information
Mark 7.6-8
Acts 19.1-7
John 5.39-40
Matt. 7.21-23

At that time, Herod the tetrarch heard about the fame of Jesus.
~ Matt. 14.1

1

Ignorance - Unfamiliarity with information due to naivete, indifference, or hardness
Eph. 4.17-19
Ps. 2.1-3
Rom. 1.21; 2.19
1 John 2.11

Who is the Lord that I should heed his voice?
~ Exod. 5.2

0

Appendix 14

The Way of Wisdom

Rev. Dr. Don L. Davis

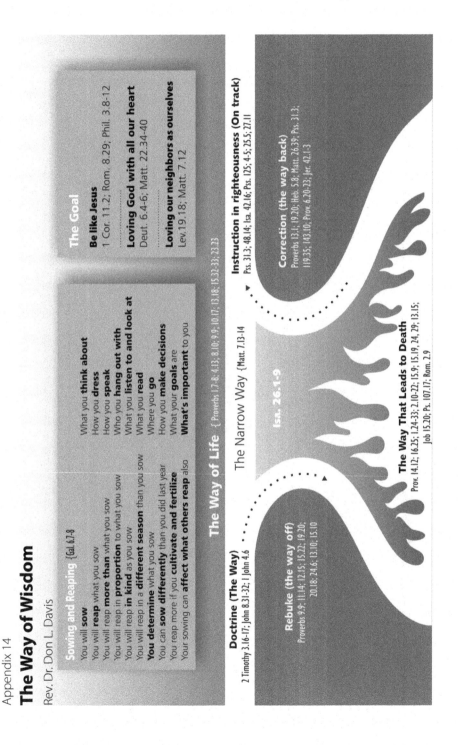

Sowing and Reaping {Gal. 6.7-8}

You will **sow**
You will **reap** what you sow
You will reap **more than** what you sow
You will reap in **proportion** to what you sow
You will reap **in kind** as you sow
You will reap in a **different season** than you sow
You determine what you sow
You can **sow differently** than you did last year
You reap more if you **cultivate and fertilize**
Your sowing can **affect what others reap** also

What you **think about**
How you **dress**
How you **speak**
Who you **hang out with**
What you **listen to and look at**
What you **read**
Where you **go**
How you **make decisions**
What your **goals** are
What's important to you

The Goal

Be like Jesus
1 Cor. 11.2; Rom. 8.29; Phil. 3.8-12

Loving God with all our heart
Deut. 6.4-6; Matt. 22.34-40

Loving our neighbors as ourselves
Lev.19.18; Matt. 7.12

The Way of Life {Proverbs 1.7-8; 4.13; 8.10; 9.9; 10.17; 13.18; 15.32-33; 23.23}

The Narrow Way {Matt. 7.13-14}

Instruction in righteousness (On track)
Pss. 31.3; 48.14; Isa. 42.16; Pss. 12.5; 4-5; 25.5; 27.11

Correction (the way back)
Proverbs 13.1; 19.20; Heb. 5.8; Matt. 26.39; Pss. 31.3; 119.35; 143.10; Prov. 6.20-23; Jer. 42.1-3

Isa. 26.1-9

Rebuke (the way off)
Proverbs 9.9; 11.14; 12.15; 15.22; 19.20; 20.18; 24.6; 13.10; 15.10

Doctrine (The Way)
2 Timothy 3.16-17; John 8.31-32; 1 John 4.6

The Way That Leads to Death
Prov. 14.12; 16.25; 1.24-33; 2.10-22; 15.9; 15.19, 24, 29; 13.15; Job 15.20; Ps. 107.17; Rom. 2.9

Appendix 15

Understanding Leadership as Representation: The Six Stages of Formal Proxy

Rev. Dr. Don L. Davis

Luke 10:1 (ESV) – After this the Lord appointed seventy-two others and sent them on ahead of him, two by two, into every town and place where he himself was about to go . . .

Luke 10:16 (ESV) – "The one who hears you hears me, and the one who rejects you rejects me, and the one who rejects me rejects him who sent me."

John 20:21 (ESV) – Jesus said to them again, "Peace be with you. As the Father has sent me, even so I am sending you."

Commissioning [1]
Formal Selection and Call to Represent
- Chosen to be an emissary, envoy, or proxy
- Confirmed by appropriate other who recognize the call
- Is recognized to be a member of a faithful community
- Calling out of a group to a particular role of representation
- Calling to a particular task or mission
- Delegation of position or responsibility

Equipping [2]
Appropriate Resourcing and Training to Fulfill the Call
- Assignment to a supervisor, superior, mentor, or instructor
- Disciplined instruction of principles underlying the call
- Constant drill, practice, and exposure to appropriate skills
- Recognition of gifts and strengths
- Expert coaching and ongoing feedback

Entrustment [3]
Corresponding Authorization and Empowerment to Act
- Delegation of authority to act and speak on commissioner's behalf
- Scope and limits of representative power provided
- Formal deputization (right to enforce and represent)
- Permission given to be an emissary (to stand in stead of)
- Release to fulfill the commission and task received

CONVICTION

CONSCIENCE

CHARACTER

Leadership As Representation

The Revealed Will of God

The Fulfillment of the Task and Mission

Consent of Your Leaders

Mission [4]
Faithful and Disciplined Engagement of the Task
- Subordination of one's will to accomplish the assignment
- Obedience: carrying out the orders of those who sent you
- Fulfilling the task that was given to you
- Freely acting within one's delegated authority to fulfill the task
- Maintaining loyalty to those who sent you
- Using all means available to do one's duty, whatever the cost
- Full recognition of one's answerability to the one(s) who commissioned

Reward [6]
Public Recognition and Continuing Response
- Formal publishing of assessment's results
- Acknowledgment and recognition of behavior and conduct
- Corresponding reward or rebuke for execution
- Review made basis for possible reassignment or recommissioning
- Assigning new projects with greater authority

Reckoning [5]
Official Evaluation and Review of One's Execution
- Reporting back to sending authority for critical review
- Formal comprehensive assessment of one's execution and results
- Judgment of one's loyalties and faithfulness
- Sensitive analysis of what we accomplished
- Readiness to ensure that our activities and efforts produce results

Appendix 16

Representin': Jesus as God's Chosen Representative

Rev. Dr. Don L. Davis

To represent another
Is to be selected to stand in the place of another, and thereby fulfill the assigned duties, exercise the rights and serve as deputy for, as well as to speak and act with another's authority on behalf of their interests and reputation.

The Temptation of Jesus Christ
Challenge to and Contention with God's Rep

Mark 1.12-13 – The Spirit immediately drove him out into the wilderness. [13] *And he was in the wilderness forty days, being tempted by Satan.* And he was with the wild animals, and the angels were ministering to him.

Jesus Fulfills The Duties Of Being an Emissary

1. Receiving an *Assignment*,
   John 10.17-18

2. Resourced with an *Entrustment*,
   John 3.34; Luke. 4.18

3. Launched into *Engagement*,
   John 5.30

4. Answered with an *Assessment*,
   Matthew 3.16-17

5. New assignment after *Assessment*,
   Philippians 2.9-11

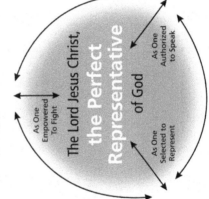

The Lord Jesus Christ, the Perfect Representative of God

As One Empowered To Fight

As One Authorized to Speak

As One Selected to Represent

The Public Preaching Ministry of Jesus Christ
Communication and Conveyance by God's Rep

Mark 1.14-15 – Now after John was arrested, Jesus came into Galilee, proclaiming the gospel of God, and saying, "The time is fulfilled, and the kingdom of God is at hand; repent and believe in the gospel."

The Baptism of Jesus Christ
Commissioning and Confirmation of God's Rep

Mark 1.9-11 – *In those days Jesus came from Nazareth of Galilee and was baptized by John in the Jordan.* [10] And when he came up out of the water, immediately he saw the heavens opening and the Spirit descending on him like a dove. [11] And a voice came from heaven, "You are my beloved Son; with you I am well pleased."

Appendix 17

Fit to Represent: Multiplying Disciples of the Kingdom of God

Rev. Dr. Don L. Davis

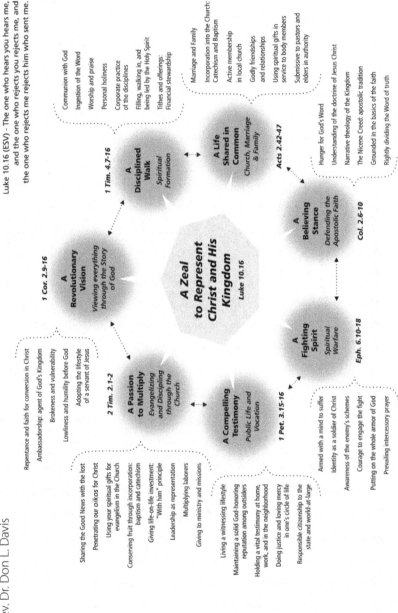

Luke 10.16 (ESV) - The one who hears you hears me, and the one who rejects you rejects me, and the one who rejects me rejects him who sent me.

A Zeal to Represent Christ and His Kingdom
Luke 10.16

A Revolutionary Vision
Viewing everything through the Story of God
1 Cor. 2.9-16

A Disciplined Walk
Spiritual Formation
1 Tim. 4.7-16

- Communion with God
- Ingestion of the Word
- Worship and praise
- Personal holiness
- Corporate practice of the disciplines
- Filling, walking in, and being led by the Holy Spirit
- Tithes and offerings: Financial stewardship

A Life Shared in Common
Church, Marriage & Family
Acts 2.42-47

- Marriage and Family
- Incorporation into the Church: Catechism and Baptism
- Active membership in local church
- Godly friendships and relationships
- Using spiritual gifts in service to body members
- Submissive to pastors and elders in authority

A Believing Stance
Defending the Apostolic Faith
Col. 2.6-10

- Hunger for God's Word
- Understanding of the doctrine of Jesus Christ
- Narrative theology of the Kingdom
- The Nicene Creed: apostolic tradition
- Grounded in the basics of the faith
- Rightly dividing the Word of truth

A Passion to Multiply
Evangelizing and Discipling through the Church
2 Tim. 2.1-2

- Repentance and faith for conversion in Christ
- Ambassadorship: agent of God's Kingdom
- Brokenness and vulnerability
- Lowliness and humility before God
- Adopting the lifestyle of a servant of Jesus

- Sharing the Good News with the lost
- Penetrating our *oikos* for Christ
- Using your spiritual gifts for evangelism in the Church
- Conserving fruit through incorporation: baptism and catechism
- Giving life-on-life investment: "With him" principle
- Leadership as representation
- Multiplying laborers
- Giving to ministry and missions

A Compelling Testimony
Public Life and Vocation
1 Pet. 3.15-16

- Living a witnessing lifestyle
- Maintaining a solid God-honoring reputation among outsiders
- Holding a vital testimony at home, work, and in the neighborhood
- Doing justice and loving mercy in one's circle of life
- Responsible citizenship to the state and world-at-large

A Fighting Spirit
Spiritual Warfare
Eph. 6.10-18

- Armed with a mind to suffer
- Identity as a soldier of Christ
- Awareness of the enemy's schemes
- Courage to engage the fight
- Putting on the whole armor of God
- Prevailing intercessory prayer

Appendix 18

The *Oikos* Factor: Spheres of Relationship and Influence

Rev. Dr. Don L. Davis

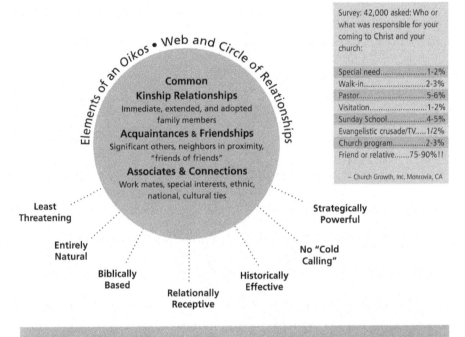

Survey: 42,000 asked: Who or what was responsible for your coming to Christ and your church:

Special need....................1-2%
Walk-in...........................2-3%
Pastor.............................5-6%
Visitation.........................1-2%
Sunday School.................4-5%
Evangelistic crusade/TV....1/2%
Church program..............2-3%
Friend or relative.......75-90%!!

~ Church Growth, Inc. Monrovia, CA

Elements of an Oikos • Web and Circle of Relationships

Common Kinship Relationships
Immediate, extended, and adopted family members

Acquaintances & Friendships
Significant others, neighbors in proximity, "friends of friends"

Associates & Connections
Work mates, special interests, ethnic, national, cultural ties

Least Threatening

Strategically Powerful

Entirely Natural

No "Cold Calling"

Biblically Based

Historically Effective

Relationally Receptive

Oikos (household) in the OT
"A household usually contained four generations, including men, married women, unmarried daughters, slaves of both sexes, persons without citizenship, and 'sojourners,' or resident foreign workers."

~ *Hans Walter Wolff, Anthology of the Old Testament*

Oikos (household) in the NT
Evangelism and disciple making in our NT narratives are often described as following the flow of the relational networks of various people within their *oikoi* (households), that is, those natural lines of connection in which they resided and lived (c.f., Mark 5.19; Luke 19.9; John 4.53; 1.41-45, etc.). Andrew to Simon (John 1.41-45), and both Cornelius (Acts 10-11) and the Philippian jailer (Acts 16) are notable cases of evangelism and discipling through *oikoi*.

Oikos (household) among the urban poor
While great differences exist between cultures, kinship relationships, special interest groups, and family structures among urban populations, it is clear that urbanites connect with others far more on the basis of connections through relationships, friendships, and family than through proximity and neighborhood alone. Often times the closest friends of urban poor dwellers are not immediately close by in terms of neighborhood; family and friends may dwell blocks, even miles away. Taking the time to study the precise linkages of relationships among the dwellers in a certain area can prove extremely helpful in determining the most effective strategies for evangelism and disciple making in inner city contexts.

Appendix 19

Living as an *Oikos* Ambassador

Rev. Dr. Don L. Davis

1
Immediate Family
• Spouse
• Children
• Parents
• Siblings

2
Relatives
• Family members
• Kinship relations
• Parents' kin
• Distant relatives

3
Close Friends
• Intimates
• Lifelong connections
• Significant others
• Romance and dating
• Experience bonds

4
Neighbors
• Those living close by
• Those in need
• "Historical" neighbors
• Those deemed such
• Sharing common experience

5
Associates
• Proximity folk
• Fellow employees
• Subordinates
• Peers and leaders
• Memberships, groups
• Affiliations
• Mutual interests

6
Acquaintances
• Somewhat familiars
• Contacts through mutual friends, family
• Connections from work
• Those "known" from frequent visits, events
• Introductions

7
Person(s) "X"
• Strangers
• Chance contacts
• Unknowns, the "others"
• Those different
• Those viewed as "unclean"
• Those considered dangerous
• Encounters in life

Living as an
oikos
Ambassador

Appendix 20
Bibliography for Further Study on
Getting Your Pretense On
Rev. Dr. Don L. Davis

Anderson, Neil T. *The Bondage Breaker*. Harvest House Publishers, Eugene, OR: 1990, 1993, 2000.

Backus, William. *Telling Teach Other the Truth*. Bethany House Publishers, Bloomington, MN: 1985.

Crabb, Dr. Larry. *Effective Biblical Counseling: A Model for Helping Caring Christians Become Capable Counselors*. Zondervan Publishing House, Grand Rapids, MI: 1977.

McGee, Robert S. *The Search for Significance: Seeing Your True Worth through God's Eyes*. Thomas Nelson, Nashville, TN: 1987, 2003.

Rothschild, Jennifer. *Self Talk, Soul Talk: What to Say When You Talk to Yourself*. Harvest House Publishers, Eugene, OR: 2007.

Thurman, Dr. Chris. *The Lies We Believe: The #1 Cause of Our Unhappiness*. Thomas Nelson Publishers, Nashville, TN: 1989.

Wright, H. Norman. *Self-talk, Imagery, and Prayer in Counseling*. Word Books Publisher, Waco, TX: 1986.

Endnotes

1   C. S. Lewis, *Mere Christianity*. New York: Macmillan Publishing Company, 1943, copyright renewed © 1980, pp. 162-63.

2   J. R. R. Tolkien. "On Fairy-Stories," in *Essays Presented to Charles Williams*, ed. by C. S. Lewis. Grand Rapids: Wm. B. Eerdmans Publishing Co., 1966), p. 81.

3   Ibid., p. 84.

4   Frederick Buechner. *Telling the Truth: The Gospel as Tragedy, Comedy, and Fairy Tale*. San Francisco: HarperSanFrancisco, 1977, p. 79-80.

5   See Appendix, *The Nicene Creed with Biblical Support*.

6   Please refer to the Appendix by Robert Webber and Philip Kenyon *A Call to An Ancient Evangelical Future* to see how the church today can rediscover the Story of the Kingdom in simple confession, worship, discipleship, and witness.

7   Please refer to the Appendix *Going Forward by Looking Back: Toward an Evangelical Retrieval of the Great Tradition*.

8   William J. Bausch, *Storytelling and Faith*. Mystic, Connecticut: Twenty-Third Publications, 1984.

9   Eugene Lowry and Frederick Buechner have both provided detailed understandings of the principle of reversal in the biblical story (see Eugene L. Lowry, *Doing Time in the Pulpit* Nashville: Abingdon Press, 1985; Frederick Buechner, *Telling the Truth: The Gospel as Tragedy, Comedy, and Fairy Tale*. San Francisco: Harper and Row, 1977). For a wonderful and rich discussion of the

principle of reversal in a homiletical context please see Ronald J. Sider and Michael A. King, *Preaching about Life in a Threatening World*. Philadelphia: The Westminster Press, 1987.

10   See Tertullian in *Against Marcion* iv 8 (*http://www.newadvent.org/ fathers/03124.htm*) on the negative ways in which Nazarenes was used, and Julian quoted in Gregory of Nazianus, *Oration* 4 (*http://www.tertullian.org/ fathers/gregory_nazianzen_2_oration4.htm*).

11   George Barna, *Revolution*. Carol Stream, IL: Tyndale House Publishers, 2005, pp. 36-37.

12   Keith Phillips, *Out of Ashes*. Los Angeles: World Impact Press, 1996, p. 131.

13   Jacques Ellul, *The Ethics of Freedom*. Translated by Geoffrey W. Bromiley, (Grand Rapids: Eerdmans, 1976), pp. 104-105.

14   J. A. Motyer *Life Application Bible Commentary*, *Ephesians*. (Electronic edition).

15   TUMI has an abundance of practical, affordable, and helpful aids to encourage you to form some good devotional and study habits in your spiritual formation as a person, a family, a small group, or even a church. For more information visit *www.tumi.org/resources*.

16   C. S. Lewis, *Mere Christianity*, p. 188.

17   The IVP *New Testament Commentary Series*, (electronic edition) *Ephesians*.

18   Please check the appendix section of this book to engage various kinds of graphics I have created over the years to help emerging leaders know its primacy in Christian leadership development. In my view, this principle is critical to discovering the core of biblical leadership, as well as a solid, exegetically sound way to make sense of what it means.

19   David Bennett, *Metaphors of Ministry*. Eugene, OR: Wiph and Stock Publishers, 2004, p. 136.

20   Ibid, p. 62.

21   Paul Tripp. "Ambassadors." *https://www.paultripp.com/articles/posts/ ambassadors-for-christ*

22   For a one page at-a-glance graphic of these principles, please see the Appendix *Understanding Leadership as Representation: The Six Stages of Formal Proxy*.

23 The upcoming chapter entitled "The *Oikos* Factor" deals specifically with the relationships (family, friends, and associates) in each of our lives that maps out the areas of our own particular calling to represent Christ in our web of influence. Everyone is called to serve as Christ's ambassador in their own unique, special, and particular arena, each of us with our own circle of contacts and relationships.

24 This cycle of mission and reward is often repeated in Jesus's parables, including the parable of the Tenants (Matt. 21.33-41), the Parable of the Wicked Tenants (Luke 20.9-19), the Parable of the Talents (Matt. 25.14-30), the parable of the Dishonest Manager (Luke 16.1-13), and the Parable of the Minas (Luke 19.12-27). The idea is that those who are faithful in little things, will receive lesser reward, and those who are faithful in great things will receive a greater reward.

25 Paul (and the apostles) referred to the reward they sought often in his writings to the churches (e.g., 1 Cor. 9.16-18, 24-25; Phil. 3.11-14; 2 Tim. 2.5; 4.6-8; James 1.12; 1 Pet. 5.4). For those who are faithful, Jesus will provide crowns of recognition and blessing, which are available to all who do his will as his representatives during their lifetimes.

26 *Oikos* is a dynamic concept in the Scriptures "The idea of household management extends to stewardship and economy (from the Greek word *oikos*, "house") and then further to "stewardship of the world," and then it becomes a word for "the world" itself. It is used in this sense, for example, in Matthew 24.14 (and Luke 2.1, 4.5; Acts 17.6; Rom. 10.18; Heb. 1.6; Rev. 16.14)." Leland Ryken. *Dictionary of Biblical Imagery.* (electronic ed.). Downers Grove, IL: InterVarsity Press, 2000. p. 394.

27 G. W. Icenogle, *Biblical Foundations for Small Group Ministry: An Integrative Approach.* Downers Grove, IL: InterVarsity Press, 1994.

28 One of the most important functions of the *oikos* when it comes to family is the ease in which we can *ground new Christians* in Christ *within the family context.* The same natural, convenient, and simple approach the *oikos* relationships provide *for evangelism*, they also provide *for follow up and spiritual formation*, which can easily be integrated within the rhythms and schedules of a family. The ability to follow the Lord together in the disciplines, in corporate worship, in reading the Scriptures, in prayer, and in following the Church Year together all reinforce in the family the power of the Story *embodied in the life of the family's practices, disciplines, and growth together.* (For a wonderfully practical and helpful guide to this kind of deep incorporation of the Christian story into the life of the family please read Winfield Bevins' *Grow at Home: A Beginner's Guide to Family Discipleship.* Franklin, Tennessee: Seedbed.com).